Family Forest Owners of the United States, 2006

A Technical Document Supporting the Forest Service 2010 RPA Assessment

Brett J. Butler

Butler, Brett J. 2008. **Family Forest Owners of the United States, 2006.** Gen. Tech. Rep. NRS-27. Newtown Square, PA: U.S. Department of Agriculture, Forest Service, Northern Research Station. 72 p.

This report summarizes results from the U.S. Forest Service's National Woodland Owner Survey of the estimated 10 million family forest owners who own 264 million acres (35 percent) of forest land in the United States. We collected information between 2002 and 2006 on family forest owners' forest holding characteristics, ownership histories, ownership objectives, forest uses, forest management practices, preferred methods for receiving information, concerns, future intentions, and demographics. National, regional, and state summary tables are included.

KEY WORDS: landowner survey, National Woodland Owner Survey, nonindustrial private forest owner

The Author

BRETT J. BUTLER, research forester, received a B.S. degree in natural resource management and engineering from the University of Connecticut in 1995 and a Ph.D. in forest science from Oregon State University in 2005. He joined the U.S. Forest Service in 1998 and the Northern Research Station's Forest Inventory and Analysis program in 2000. He coordinates the U.S. Forest Service's National Woodland Owner Survey and co-leads the Family Forest Research Center collocated with the University of Massachusetts-Amherst in Amherst, MA.

CONTENTS

EXECUTIVE SUMMARY

- An estimated 11 million private forest owners (± 3 percent) collectively control 56 percent of the forest land (423 million acres ± 0.4 percent) in the United States.

- Family forest owners account for 92 percent of the private forest owners and 62 percent of the private forest land (35 percent of all forest land) in the United States.

- Sixty-one percent of family forest owners in the United States own less than 10 acres of forest land, but 53 percent of the family forest land is owned by people with 100 or more acres.

- The average (mean) land tenure for family forest owners is 26 years.

- Most family forest owners own their forest land for multiple reasons. The most commonly cited reasons are beauty/scenery, to pass land on to heirs, privacy, nature protection, and part of home/cabin.

- Two out of every 5 acres of family forest land are owned by absentee owners.

- Fifty-eight percent of family forest land is owned by people who have commercially harvested trees.

- One in 5 acres of family forest land is owned by someone who has a written forest management plan. Two in 5 acres is owned by someone who has received forest management advice. The most common sources of this advice are state forestry agencies and private consultants.

- Issues most commonly rated as major concerns by family forest owners are insects and plant diseases, keeping land intact for heirs, fire, trespassing, and property taxes.

- Most family forest owners plan to do relatively little with their forest land in the next 5 years. Of those who intend to actively do something with their land, harvesting sawlogs or pulpwood and harvesting firewood are the most commonly planned activities. One in 5 acres is owned by someone who plans to sell or transfer some or all of their forest land in the next 5 years.

- Compared to the general population, there are a greater proportion of family forest owners who are older, white, male, more educated, and wealthier. One in 5 acres of forest land is owned by someone who is at least 75 years of age.

INTRODUCTION

The National Woodland Owner Survey (NWOS) is conducted by the Forest Service, U.S. Department of Agriculture, Forest Inventory and Analysis (FIA) program to characterize the private forest owners of the United States. It is the social compliment to the biophysical surveys FIA conducts. Previous national surveys of private forest owners, with varying levels of details and comparability (see sidebar), were conducted by Birch (1996a), Birch et al. (1982), and Josephson and McGuire (1958).

Family forest owners are the focus of this publication. Limited information for all forest lands, private and public, is included to provide a broader context and to aid comparisons with other studies. Family forest owners, forest land, and other pertinent terms are defined in the "Key Definitions" sidebar. The basic relationships of the ownership categories used in this report are summarized in Figure 1.

This publication summarizes the responses from 15,440 family forest owners (Table A)[1] who participated in the NWOS between 2002 and 2006. The over-all cooperation rate for the NWOS is 51.3 percent. As described briefly in Appendix I: Data and Methods and in full detail in Butler et al. (2005), the NWOS has been implemented on an annual basis since 2002; the 2002-2006 data reported here represents the first 5-year cycle of data collected under this new system. The nominal date assigned to these data is 2006. The underlying forest area estimates are derived from the 2007 Renewable Resources Planning Act (RPA) database compiled by FIA for the Forest Resources of the United States, 2007 report (Smith et al., in press).

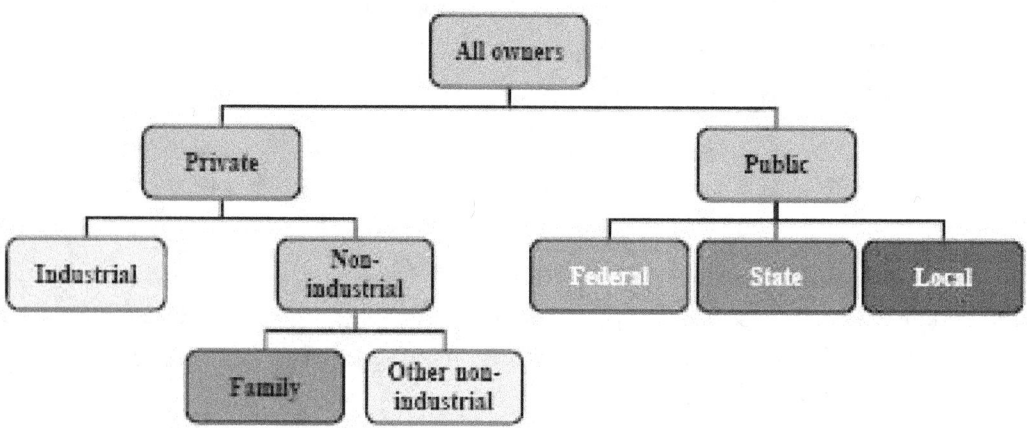

Figure 1.—Ownership categorization used in this report. Colors correspond to the categories used in Figure 4.

---

[1] All tables referred to in the printed portion of this report can be found beginning on page 39.

Assessing Trends

Although similar methods were used in the 1993 (Birch 1996a) and 2006 national forest owner surveys, analyzing trends between the two are hampered by:

- A lack of documentation of the 1993 forest area statistics that underlie all other statistics
- The 1993 study focuses on all private forest owners; this study focuses on family forest owners
- Additions, subtractions, and changes to questions asked
- Large sampling errors associated with owners of 1 to 9 acres of forest land
- Large sampling errors associated with states with small sample sizes

The implications of these issues are:

- The base 1993 forest area numbers do not always agree with other concurrent estimates (e.g., Powell et al. 1994). To resolve this problem would require rerunning the 1993 numbers using either ratio estimation procedures or, ideally, calculating new inclusion probabilities.
- Either the results from the 1993 survey must be subset to include only family forest owners or the 2006 results need to be expanded. Both approaches have benefits and shortcomings, including data limitations, that need to be further assessed.
- Although continuity over time was important in designing the 2006 survey, conscious decisions were made to improve it. The wording and structure of the questions must be considered.
- Trend comparisons excluding owners with 1 to 9 acres are more precise.
- The reliability of estimates derived from small sample sizes are questionable, sampling errors need to be assessed, and, where necessary, larger geographic areas examined.

We strongly caution anyone wishing to make direct comparisons between the 1993 and 2006 results. We are currently developing methods to overcome the shortcomings listed above and will make trend data available as soon as possible.

Key Definitions

Forest land—Land at least 10 percent stocked by forest trees of any size, including land that formerly had such tree cover and that will be naturally or artificially regenerated. The minimum area for classification of forest land is 1 acre (Smith et al. 2004).

Private forest owners—Families, individuals, corporations, and other private groups that own forest land.

Forest industry owners—Corporations and other private groups that own forest land and own and operate primary wood-processing facilities. This group is a subset of private forest owners.

Nonindustrial private forest owners—Families and individuals who own forest land and corporations and other private groups that own forest land, but do not own and operate a primary wood-processing facility. This group is a subset of private forest owners.

Family forest owners—Families, individuals, trusts, estates, family partnerships, and other unincorporated groups of individuals that own forest land. This group is a subset of nonindustrial private forest owners.

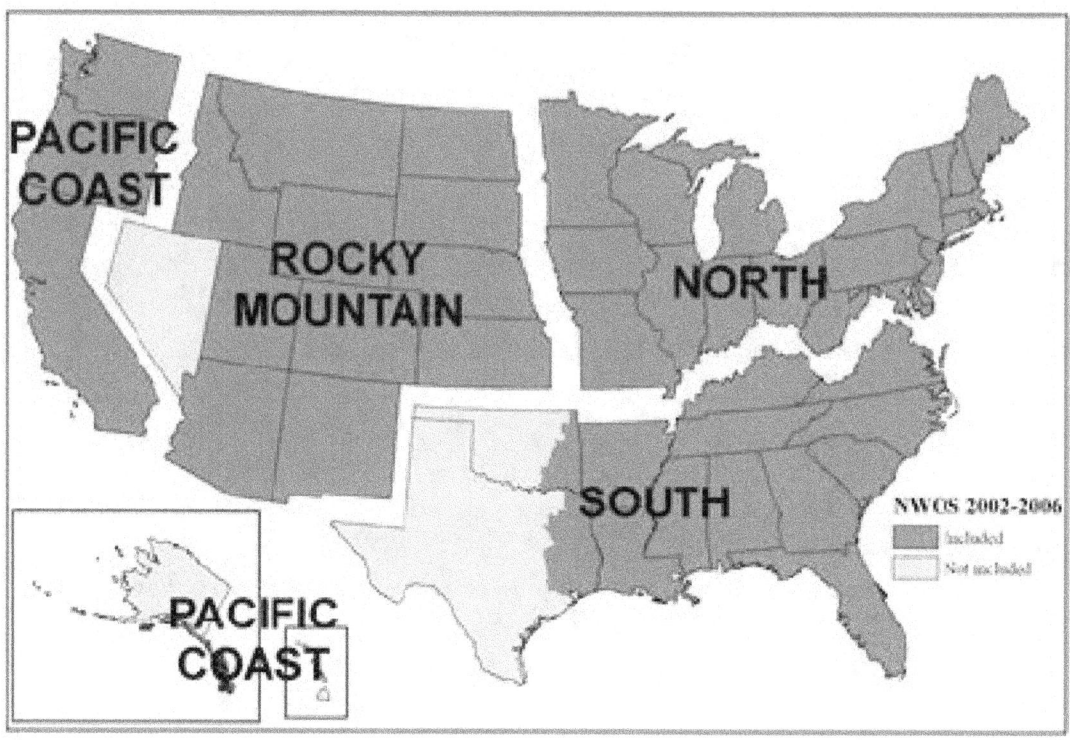

Figure 2.—Areas included in the National Woodland Owner Survey between 2002 and 2006 and delineation of multi-state analysis regions.

This report primarily focuses on national level results, but regional (Fig. 2) and state data also are included. Within a given geographic area, the tables are arranged in the same order as the corresponding questions in the NWOS questionnaire (Butler et al. 2005).

Except for Tables A and B, results are presented in terms of numbers of owners and area of forest land. These two ways of looking at the data often show different, and sometimes divergent, patterns. Both approaches are legitimate and the appropriate choice depends on one's objectives. For example, land managers interested in the prospective impact of policies on the landscape would be most interested in the area estimates. Managers interested in the number, and hence political power, of private owners impacted by policies would need to know the number of owners potentially impacted. In addition, some will want to consider only certain segments of family forest owners (e.g., owners with forest holdings of 10 to 999 acres). This, too, is perfectly reasonable, but the number of permutations that people may want to examine is nearly infinite and for simplicity's sake, the family forest owner results presented here are for owners with 1 or more acres of forest land. The "Size of Forest Holdings Matter" sidebars highlight the relationships between the size of forest holdings and selected attributes.

No data were collected for interior Alaska, Hawaii, Nevada, western Oklahoma, or western Texas between 2002 and 2006 (Fig. 2). Nor were data colleted for Puerto Rico, the U.S. Virgin Islands, Guam, or any other U.S. territories or protectorates. The usual sampling frames for these areas were lacking; it is anticipated that during the next 5-year iteration of the NWOS, the coverage will be expanded to cover all parts of all states. During this same period, planning for implementation in the U.S. territories and protectorates will commence. Data for interior

Owners vs. Area

Forest ownership statistics can be analyzed in terms of owners or area. For example, in absolute terms:

- There are 6.2 million family forest owners (± 4 percent) with forest holdings of 1 to 9 acres in the United States (Table US-5)
- There are 19.2 million acres of forest land (± 6 percent) that are owned by family forest owners with forest holdings of 1 to 9 acres in the United States (Table US-5)

Equivalently, in relative terms:

- Sixty-one percent of the family forest owners in the United States have forest holdings of 1 to 9 acres
- Eight percent of the family forest land in the United States is owned by people with forest holdings of 1 to 9 acres

Tables in this report include summaries in terms of both owners and area. Data users should choose the summaries that are most useful to them—this may require examining owner, area, or owner and area statistics.

Alaska, Hawaii, Nevada, western Oklahoma, and western Texas are included in Tables B to E using data from Birch (1996c, 1996d) as described below, but are not included in any other tables.

The NWOS population estimates, such as numbers of family forest owners in a state, are just that – estimates. These estimates come from a systematic, random sample so the sampling frame is unbiased, but because not all owners are included (i.e., a complete enumeration is not conducted), sampling errors exist. Sampling errors are reported for all estimates in this publication and the "Sampling Errors" sidebar provides a primer on how to interpret them. Appendix I: Data and Methods contains, among other things, information on the methods used to minimize sampling and other potential survey-related errors.

The stated precision goal of the NWOS is a sampling error of 15 percent or lower for estimates of the number of family forest owners in a state (Butler et al. 2005). This will require minimum sample sizes of approximately 250. This goal has yet to be achieved in all states (Fig. 3, Table A). Sampling errors are relatively large for states with sample sizes significantly lower than the target size. Data users are strongly encouraged to examine the sample sizes and sampling errors to assess the precision of the estimates. If the precision level is lower than a data user desires, larger geographic areas should be examined.

As an annual survey, the NWOS is continually collecting and compiling new data. We plan to publish reports similar to this one every 5 years or so. An online data summary tool has been developed to provide access to the most up-to-date information and for the generation of customized NWOS tables. The latest NWOS results and information can be accessed at: www.fia.fs.fed.us/nwos.

Sampling Errors

Sampling errors arise when not all members of a population are surveyed. Sampling errors are included for all estimates in this report. They are reported in percentage terms and represent the 68 percent confidence level. For example, there are an estimated 10,398 thousand family forest owners in the United States and the sampling error associated with this estimate is 2.6 percent (Table E). This means that 68 percent of randomly selected samples will produce estimates between 10,124 and 10,671, or 10,398 ± 274. This range is referred to as a confidence interval. Stated another way, we are 68 percent confident that the true population estimate is between 10,124 and 10,671. The 68 percent confidence level is equivalent to one standard deviation and is the traditional level for reporting sampling errors. Confidence levels can be adjusted to meet users' needs. For example, multiply sample errors by 2 to calculate 95 percent confidence intervals. When examining sampling errors in this report, the following general guidance can be used:

Sampling error	Implications
< 25%	Sampling errors should be considered when interpreting results.
25% - 49%	Sampling errors should be considered when interpreting results and estimates should be used cautiously.
≥ 50%	Sampling errors should be considered when interpreting results and estimates should be used very cautiously.

Appendix I: Data and Methods of this report describes how the sampling errors were calculated.

Figure 3.—Number of family forest owners who participated in (i.e., responded to) the National Woodland Owner Survey between 2002 and 2006.

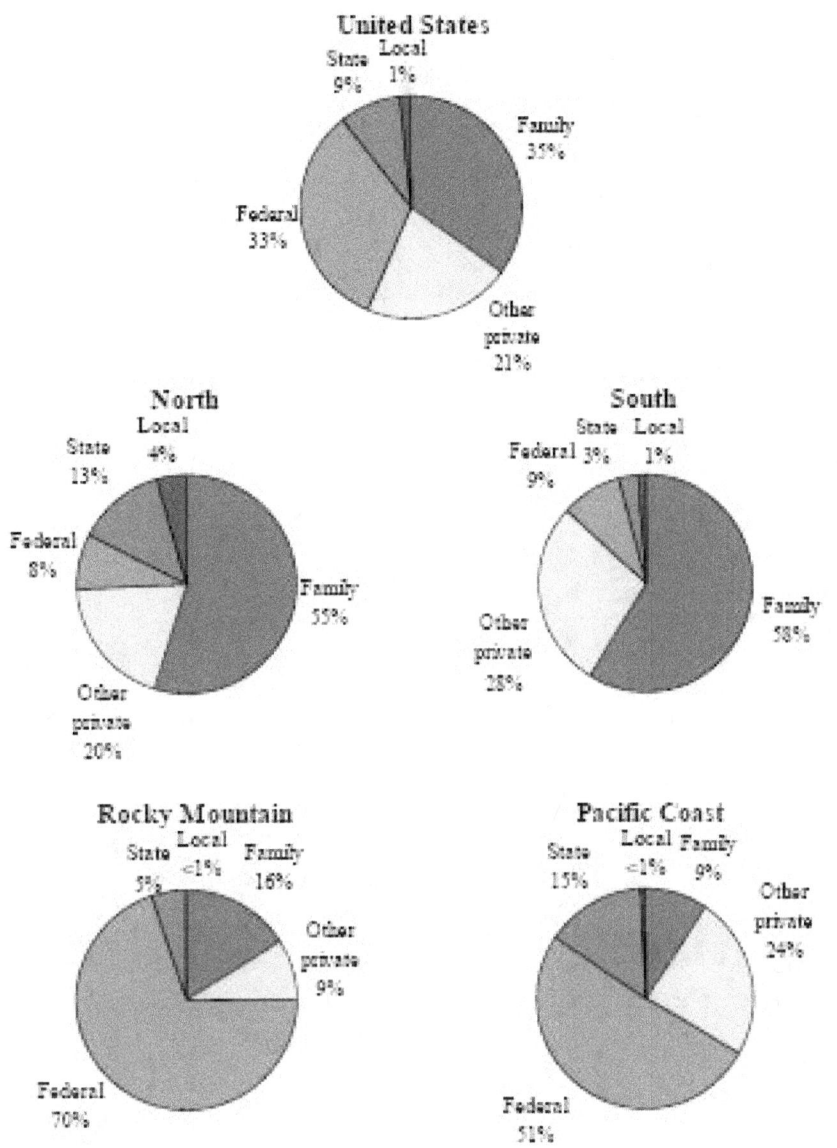

Figure 4.—Area of forest land in the United States by ownership and region, 2006.

FINDINGS

General Ownership Patterns and Trends

An estimated 11 million private forest owners (± 3 percent) collectively control 56 percent of the forest land (423 million acres ± 0.4 percent) in the United States (Fig. 4, Tables B and C). The percentage of forest land that is privately owned varies widely across the nation (Figs. 5 and 6) from a low of 2 percent in Nevada to a high of 95 percent in Kansas. Most of the private forest land is located in the southern and northern United States and so, too, are most of the private forest owners. Forty-four percent of the nation's private forest land and 44 percent of the private forest owners are in the South. The North has 30 percent of the nation's private forest land and 44 percent of the private forest owners. The states with the largest areas of private forest land, each with more than 15 million acres, are Alaska, Georgia, Alabama, Mississippi, Maine, Texas, North Carolina, and Arkansas (Fig. 6A). The states with the highest percentages of private forest ownership, each with at least 90 percent, are Kansas, Texas, Maine, Alabama, Delaware, Oklahoma, and Georgia. The states with the greatest numbers of private owners, each with more than 500,000, are New York, Tennessee, North Carolina, Georgia, and Florida (Fig. 6B).

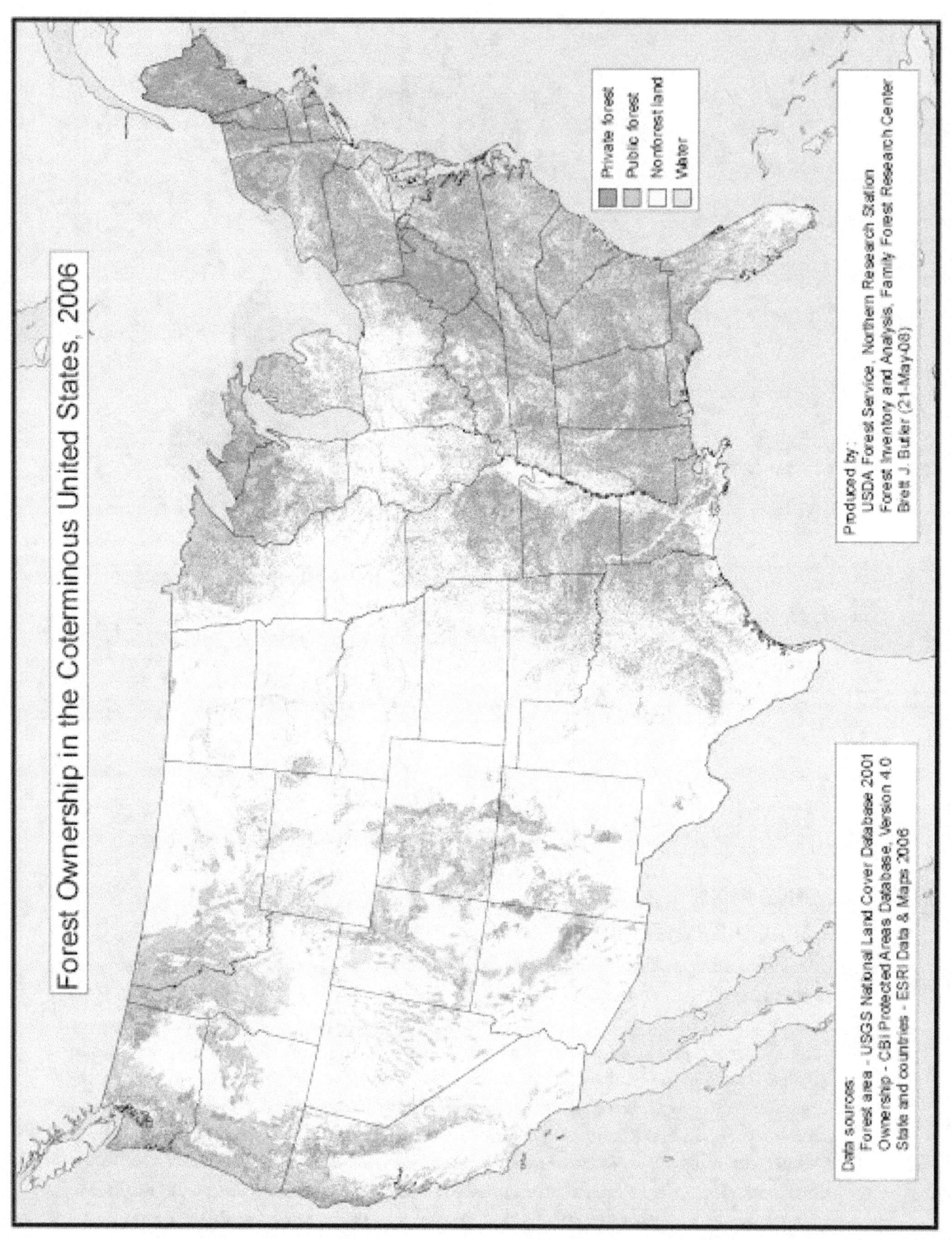

Forest Ownership in the Coterminous United States, 2006

Private forest
Public forest
Nonforest land
Water

Produced by:
USDA Forest Service, Northern Research Station
Forest Inventory and Analysis, Family Forest Research Center
Brett J. Butler (21-May-08)

Data sources:
Forest area - USGS National Land Cover Database 2001
Ownership - CBI Protected Areas Database, Version 4.0
State and countries - ESRI Data & Maps 2006

Figure 5.—Private and public forest land in the United States. An electronic version of this map is available on the CD in the back of this publication.

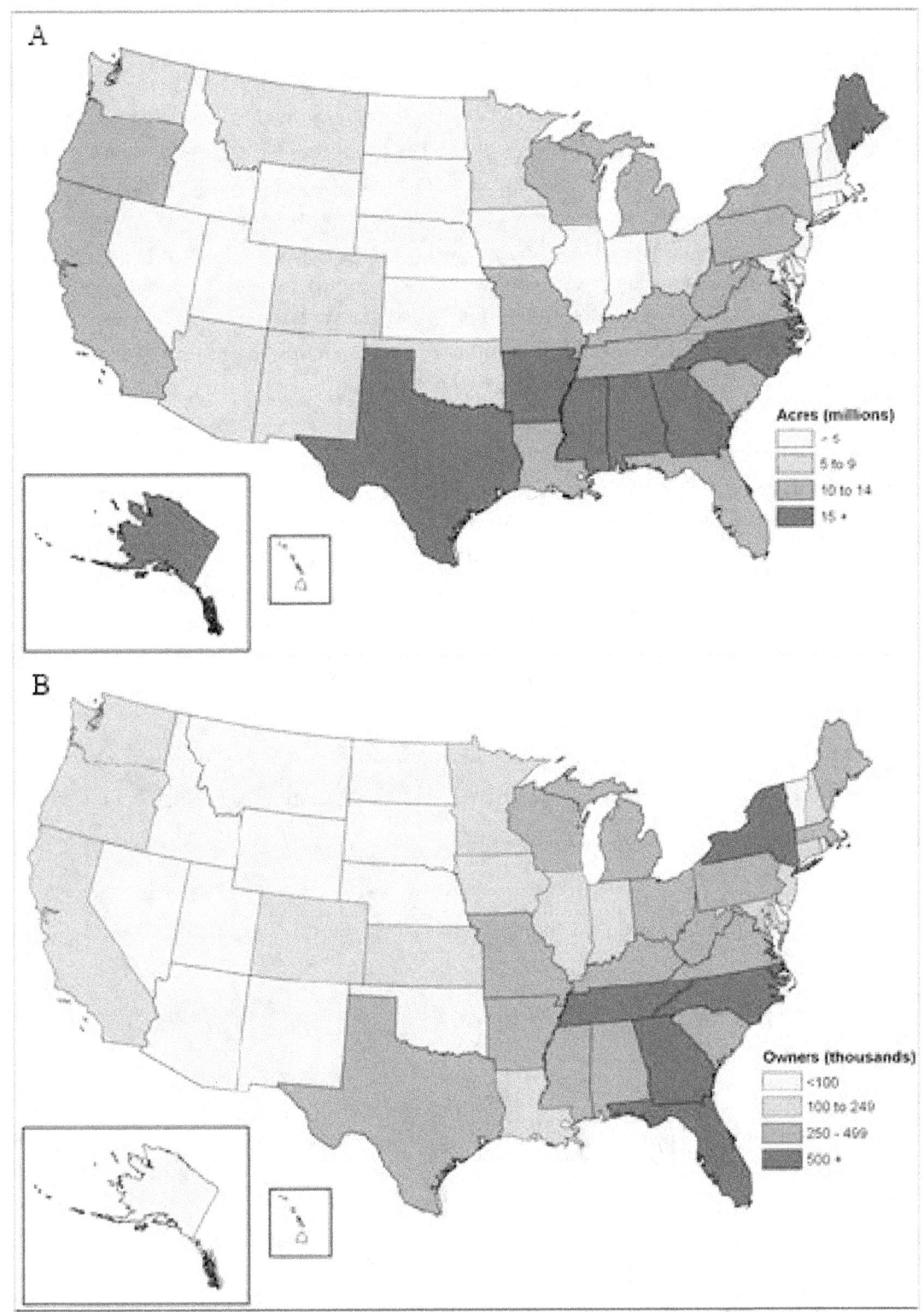

Figure 6.—(A) Area of private forests, and (B) number of private forests owners in the United States, 2006.

Nationally, family forest owners dominate the private forest owner category in terms of acres (Fig. 4) and numbers of owners. Ninety-two percent of the private forest owners were classified as family forest owners (Tables C and E). Thirty-five percent of all forest land in the United States is owned by families and individuals (Table B); in the coterminous United States, this percentage increases to 42 percent. In the major timber-producing regions of the country, forest industry and forest management companies, including timber investment management organizations (TIMOs) and timber-oriented real estate investment trusts (REITs), control most of the "other private" forest land. In other parts of the country, land conservation groups, real estate companies, and other private corporations and groups, control much of the "other private" forest land. The large-scale divestiture of forest industry lands over the past decade and the related increases of TIMO and REIT holdings is a major change in private forest ownership in the United States, but is outside the scope of this report.

Family Forest Owners

Nationally, there are 10.4 million family forest owners (± 3 percent) who own 264 million acres of forest land (± 0.4 percent) (Table E). Due to the lack of ownership survey data being collected in interior Alaska, Hawaii, Nevada, western Oklahoma, and western Texas noted previously (Fig. 2), national tables and the Southern, Rocky Mountain, and Pacific Coast regional tables exclude these areas. This makes the reference population for the national tables the 10.2 million family forest owners (± 3 percent) who own 252 million acres (± 0.4 percent) (Table US-5).

Size of Forest Holdings

Most family forest owners in the United States own less than 10 acres of forest land, but 53 percent of the family forest land is owned by people with 100 or more acres (Fig. 7, Table US-5).

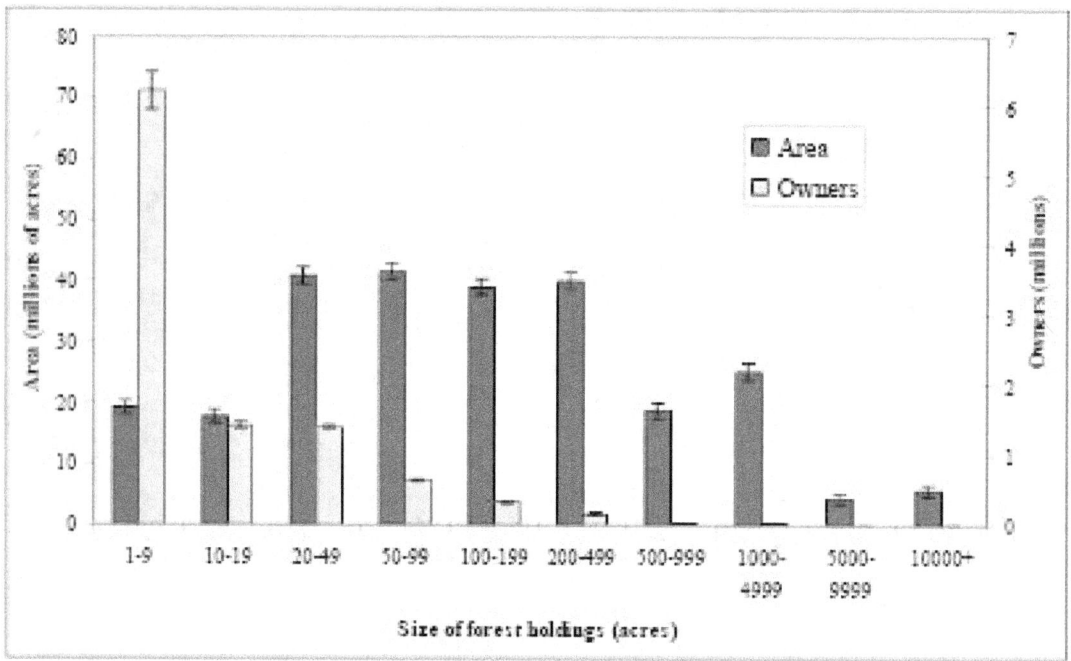

Figure 7.—Size of family forest owners' forest holdings in the United States, 2006. Error bars represent 68 percent confidence intervals.

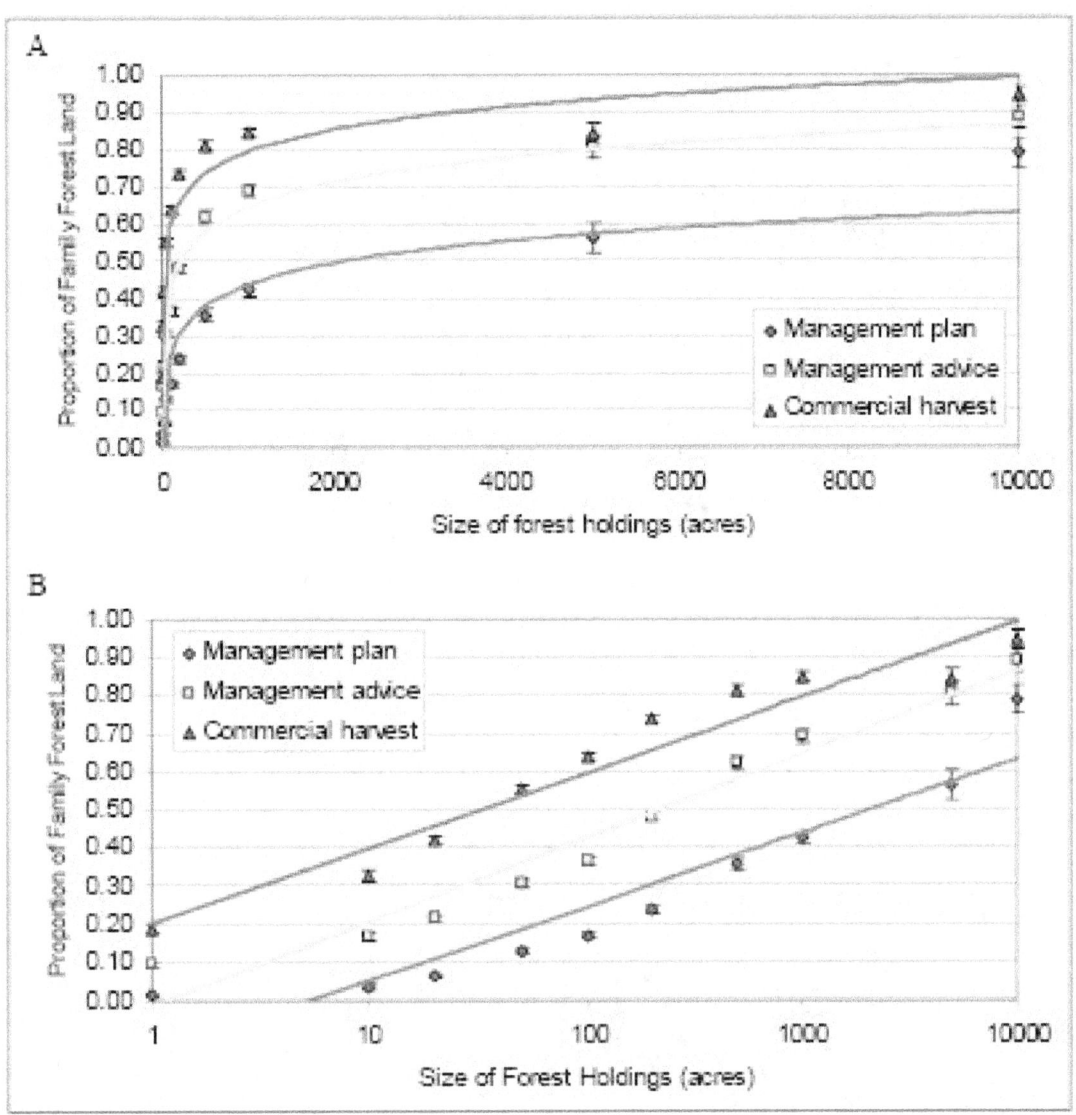

Figure 8.—Relationships between size of forest holdings and timber harvesting, forest management plans, and forest management advice for family forest owners in the United States, 2006. The x axis in Figure 8A is an arithmetic scale and in Figure 8B it is a logarithmic scale. Error bars represent 68 percent confidence intervals.

Size of forest holdings is highly correlated with many of the behaviors and attitudes of family forest owners (Fig. 8). Interspersed throughout this report are "Size of Forest Holdings Matter" sidebars that highlight differences among owners by size of forest holdings.

Nationally, the average size of family forest holdings is 25 acres. This ranges from an average of 6 acres in Rhode Island to 96 acres in Montana (Fig. 9A). Excluding owners with less than 10 acres of forest land, the average holding size increases to 58 acres with a low of 25 acres in Delaware and a high of 406 acres in New Mexico (Fig. 9B). Average forest holdings tend to be smaller in the North, particularly between Massachusetts and Maryland, and larger in the Intermountain region.

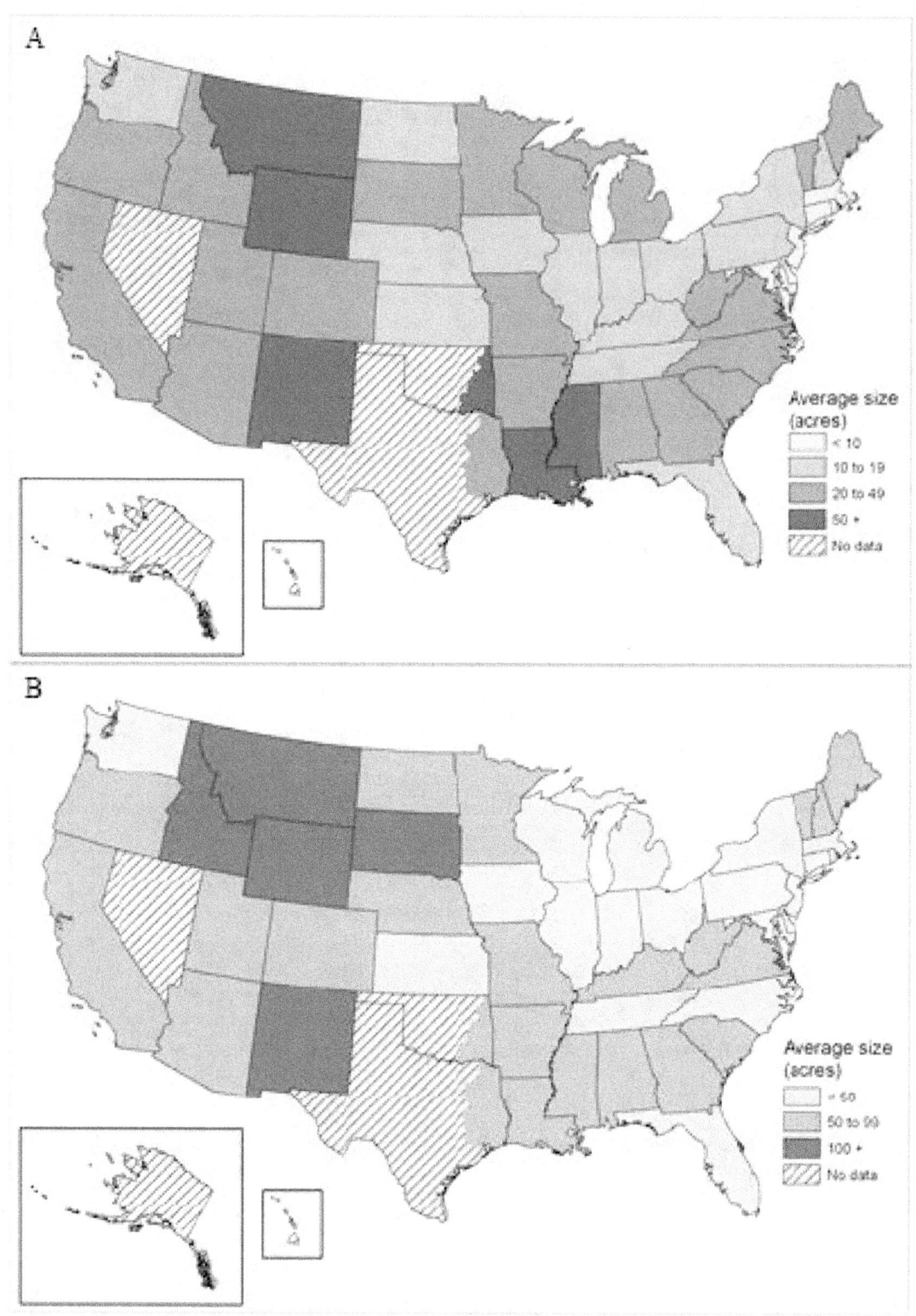

Figure 9.—Average size of family forest holdings for owners with (A) 1 or more acres of forest land, and (B) 10 or more acres of forest land in the Unites States, 2006.

Does the Size of Forest Holdings Matter?

As illustrated in Figure 8, size of forest holdings can be highly correlated with family forest owner characteristics. In this publication, "Size of Forest Holdings Matter" sidebars highlight selected attributes as functions of the size of forest holdings. The five size categories and area and number of family forests in each category are:

Size of forest landholdings	Area		Ownerships	
	Acres	Sampling error	Number	Sampling error
Acres	Thousands	Percent	Thousands	Percent
1-9	19,158	6.4	6,220	4.4
10-49	58,585	3.1	2,831	2.2
50-99	41,562	3.2	644	2.3
100-999	97,667	2.5	508	2.1
1,000+	35,003	5.6	19	8.3

The "Size of Forest Holdings Matter" sidebars show the percentage of the owners and forest land with various attributes. The numbers following the bars are the actual percentages. The estimated area of forest land or number of owners represented by each bar can be calculated by multiplying the percentage listed by the base sizes above. Interior Alaska, Hawaii, Nevada, western Oklahoma, and western Texas are not included in the base sizes above or any of the "Size of Forest Holdings Matter" figures.

Percent of Owner's Land that is Forested and Number of Parcels

The total land holdings of 19 percent[2] of family forest owners, who own 19 percent of the family forest land, is completely forested (Table US-6). Forty percent of family forest owners, who own 52 percent of the family forest land, own land that is 50 to 99 percent forested. The other 41 percent of family forest owners, who own 29 percent of the family forest land, own land that is less than 50 percent forested.

Two-thirds of the family forest owners, who own 42 percent of the family forest land, have all of their forest land in a single, contiguous parcel (Table US-7). Thirty-three percent of the owners, who own 50 percent of the family forest land, have 2 to 9 parcels of forest land. The other 1 percent of the family forest owners, who own 8 percent of the family forest land, have 10 or more parcels of forest land.

Ownership Types, Tenure, and History

Most (93 percent) family forest owners own some or all of their land either individually or jointly; collectively, they own 84 percent of the family forest land (Table US-11). Other relatively common forms of ownership are family partnerships, 6 percent of the family forest

---

[2]All percentages exclude owners who did not answer the specific question (i.e., item nonresponse).

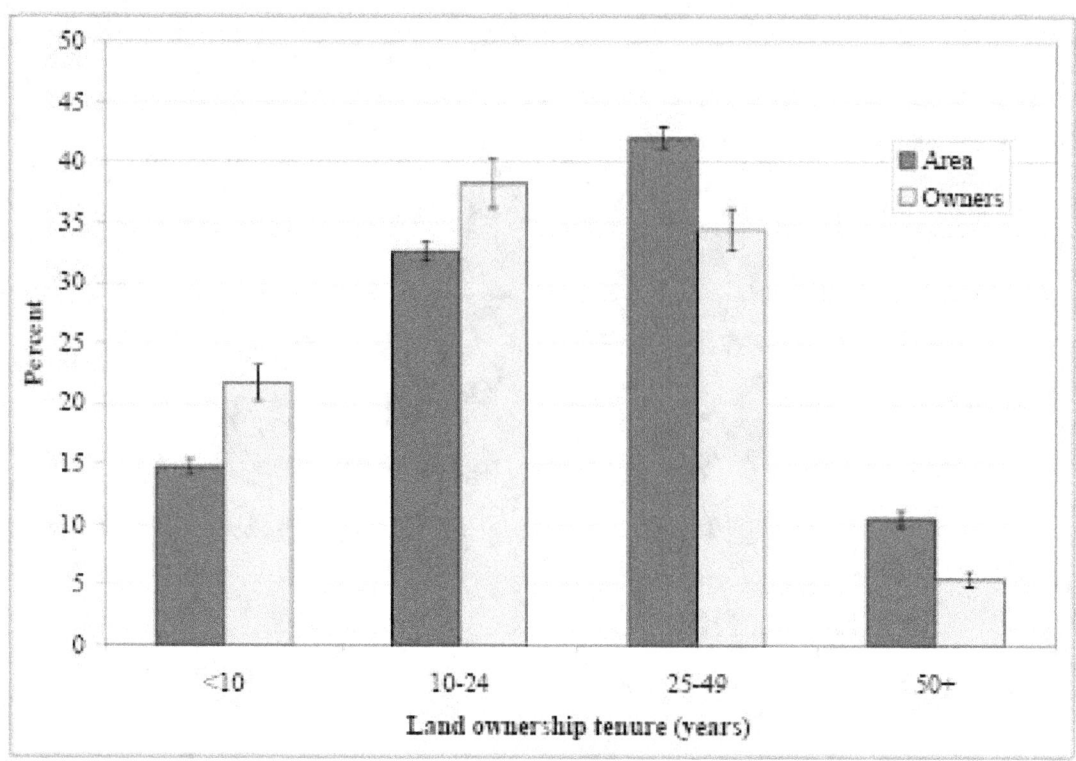

Figure 10.—Land tenure of family forest owners in the United States, 2006. Error bars represent 68 percent confidence intervals.

owners who own 16 percent of the family forest land; and trusts and estates, 4 percent of the family forest owners who own 9 percent of the family forest land. These percentages sum to more than 100 because some owners own different portions of their forest land under different legal arrangements.

Purchasing land is the most common method for forest land acquisition, but inheritance is also relatively common (Table US-8). Eighty-two percent of the family forest owners, who own 78 percent of the family forest land, purchased some or all of their forest land. Twenty percent of the owners, who own 36 percent of the family forest land, inherited some or all of their land. Most received their land from a nonfamily member, but only slightly less either purchased it or inherited it from a family member.

Most family forest owners have owned their land for relatively long periods of time (Fig. 10, Table US-9). Forty percent of the owners, who own 53 percent of the family forest land, have owned their land for 25 years or more. The average (mean) land tenure is 26 years.

Although most owners have owned land for relatively long periods of time, 24 percent of the family forest owners, who own 33 percent of the family forest land, have sold, passed on, or otherwise transferred some of it (Table US-10). Not surprisingly, owners with larger land holdings are more likely to have transferred land (see sidebar).

Size of Forest Holdings Matter: Land Tenure and Land Transfers

Percentage of family forest land and family forest owners who (A) have owned their forest land for at least 25 years, and (B) have transferred some of their forest land to other owners, by size of forest holdings.

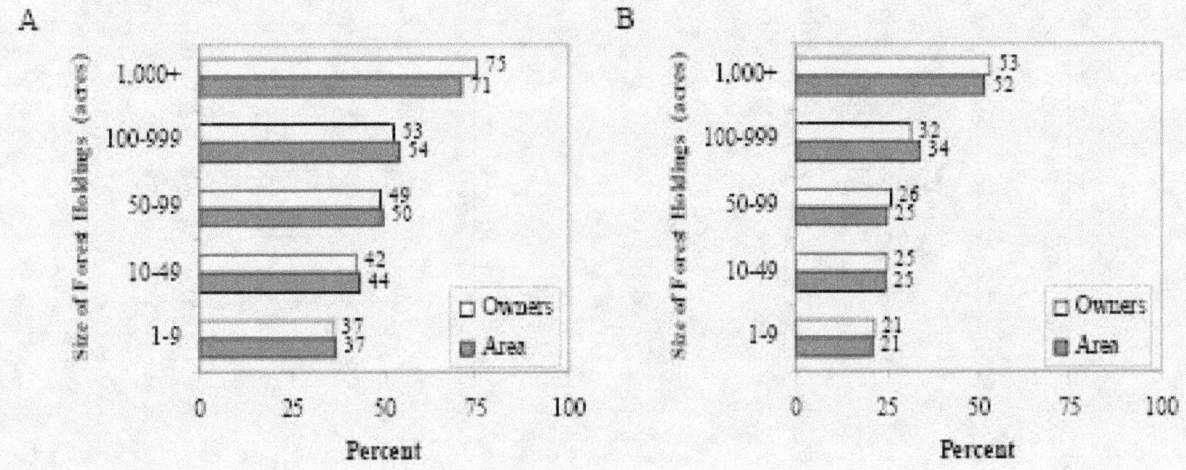

Reasons for Owning Forest Land

The reasons for owning forest land vary appreciably among family forest owners but a common trend is that most owners have multiple objectives. The NWOS asked respondents to rate 12 potential reasons for owning forest land. At least half of the family forest land is owned by people who rated beauty/scenery, passing land on to heirs, privacy, nature protection, and part of home/cabin as important or very important[3] (Fig. 11, Table US-13). Of the financial objectives they were asked to rate, land investment was rated as important or very important by 38 percent of the family forest owners, who own 47 percent of the family forest land. Timber production was rated as important or very important by 10 percent of the family forest owners, who own 32 percent of the family forest land.

Forest Land as Part of a Primary Home, Secondary Home, or Farm

Related to these ownership objectives, it is not surprising that most family forest owners, 73 percent of the family forest owners who own 59 percent of the family forest land, have their primary residence on or near (within 1 mile) their forest land (Table US-12). Secondary residences (e.g., vacation homes or cabins) are less common, but owners with secondary residences associated with their land, 12 percent of the family forest owners who control 22 percent of the family forest land, still control a large amount of land: 48.8 million acres (± 3 percent).

---

[3]Very important and important refers to values of 1 and 2, respectively, on a seven-point Likert scale with 1 defined as very important and 7 defined as not important.

Size of Forest Holdings Matter: Ownership Objectives

Percentage of family forest land and family forest owners who rated (A) timber production, and (B) enjoyment of beauty and scenery as very important or important reasons for owning their forest land, by size of forest holdings.

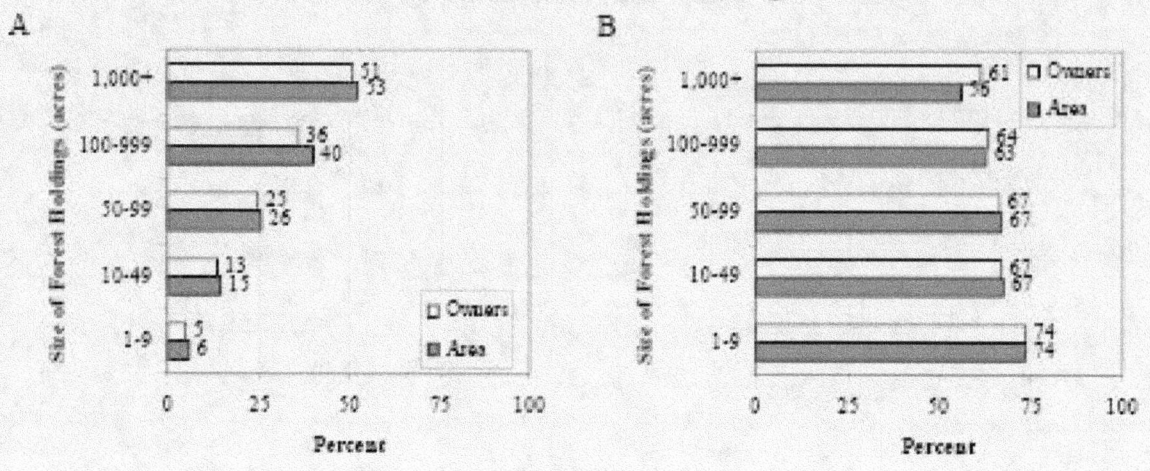

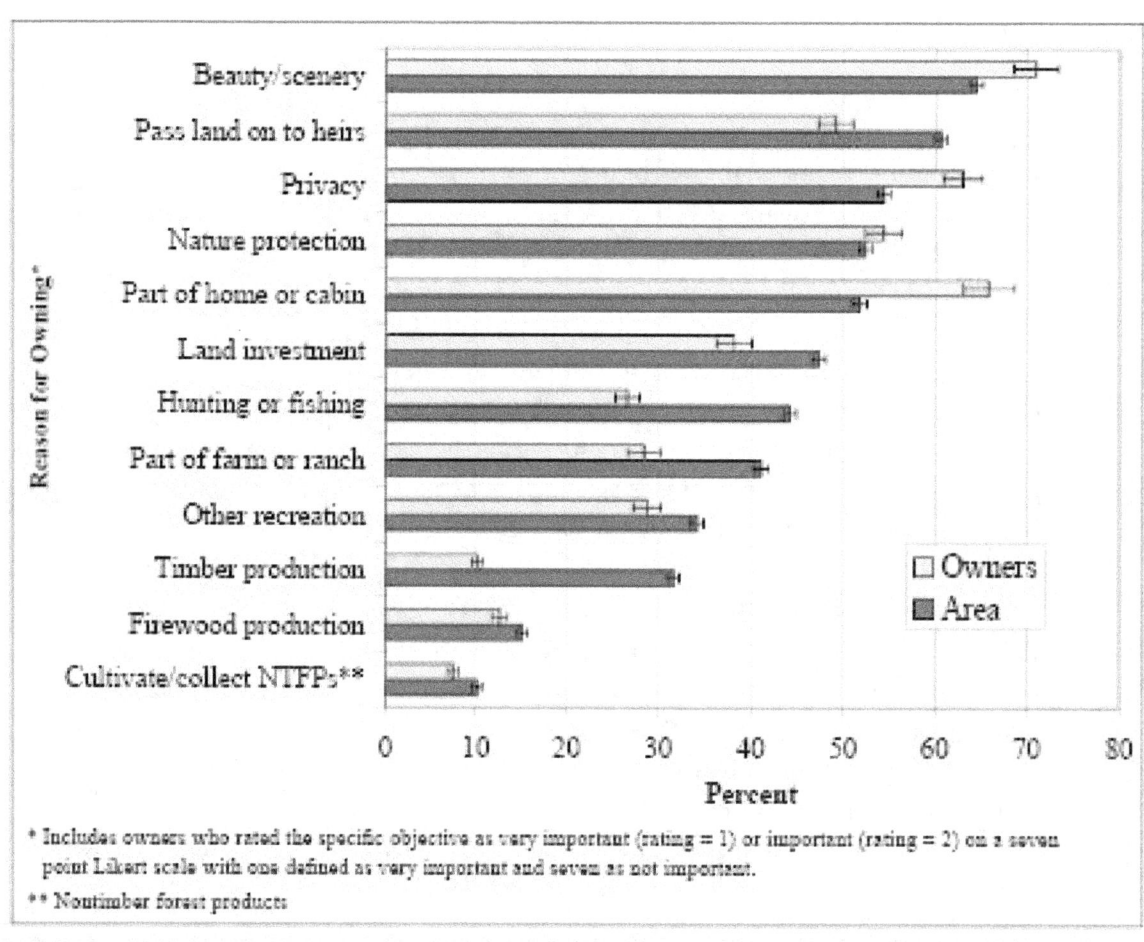

Figure 11.—Reasons for owning family forests in the United States, 2006. Error bars represent 68 percent confidence intervals.

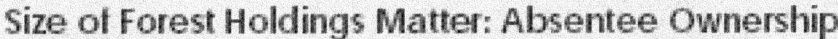

Size of Forest Holdings Matter: Absentee Ownership

Percentage of family forest land and family forest owners who do not live on or near (within one mile) their forest land, by size of forest holdings.

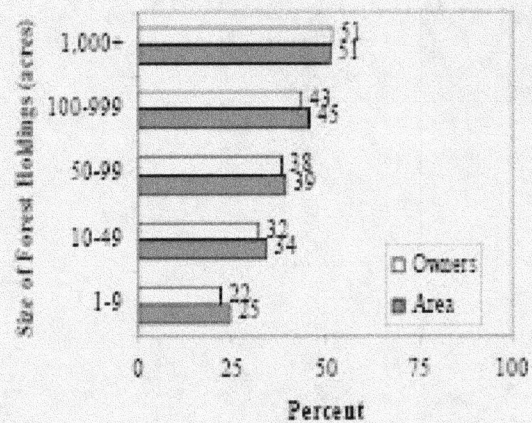

One-quarter of the family forest owners, who own 41 percent of the family forest land, reported that their land is associated with a farm or ranch (Table US-12). This equates to 2.4 million family forest owners (± 5 percent) and 100 million acres of forest land (±2 percent). From an occupational perspective, 5 percent of the family forest owners, who own 10 percent of the family forest land, reported that their primary occupation is a farmer (Table US-28). This equates to 445 thousand family forest owners (± 23 percent) and 22 million acres of forest land (± 7 percent). The National Agricultural Statistics Service (2004) reported that there were 818,000 farms owning a total of 76 million acres of "woodland" in 2002. These differences deserve further investigation, but are likely related to how leased land and gentleman/gentlewoman/hobby farms are reported, the definitions of woodland and farmland, and the inclusion or exclusion of corporate and other nonfamily owned farms. Regardless of the specific statistics, a significant amount of U.S. forest land is associated with farms.

Leasing of Forest Land

Five percent of the family forest owners, who own 23 percent of the family forest land, have leased their forest land (Table US-14). Hunting and grazing are the most common lease activities. Both the relative proportions of family forest land being leased and the purposes of these leases vary considerably across the country (Fig. 12). In the North, where leases are least common, recreation is the most common purpose for leasing. In the South, most leases are for hunting. Grazing is the most common lease activity in the Rocky Mountain and Pacific Coast regions.

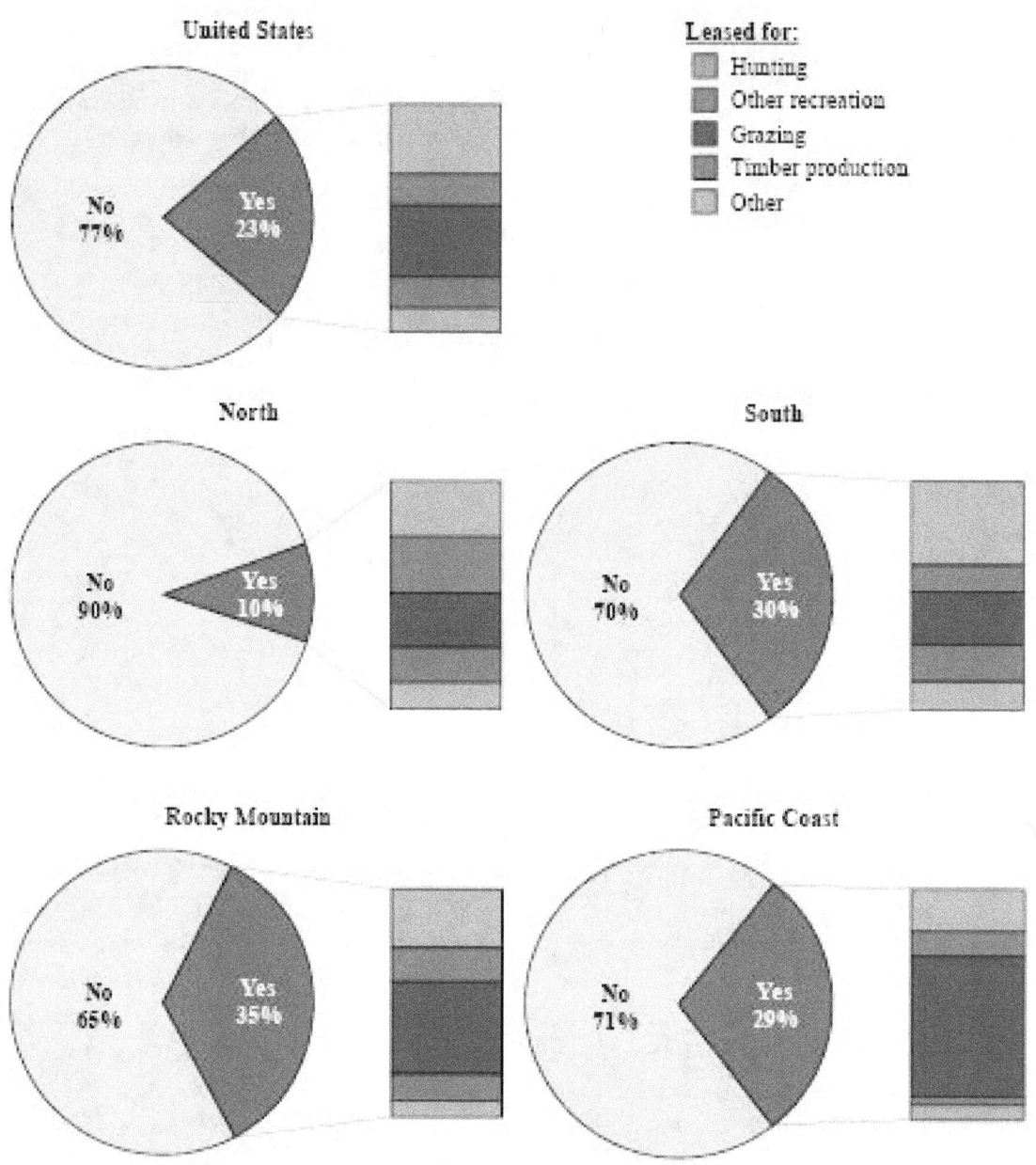

* Percentages are in terms of family forest land.

Figure 12.—Leasing of forest land and relative frequency of lease activities by family forest owners in the United States by region, 2006*.

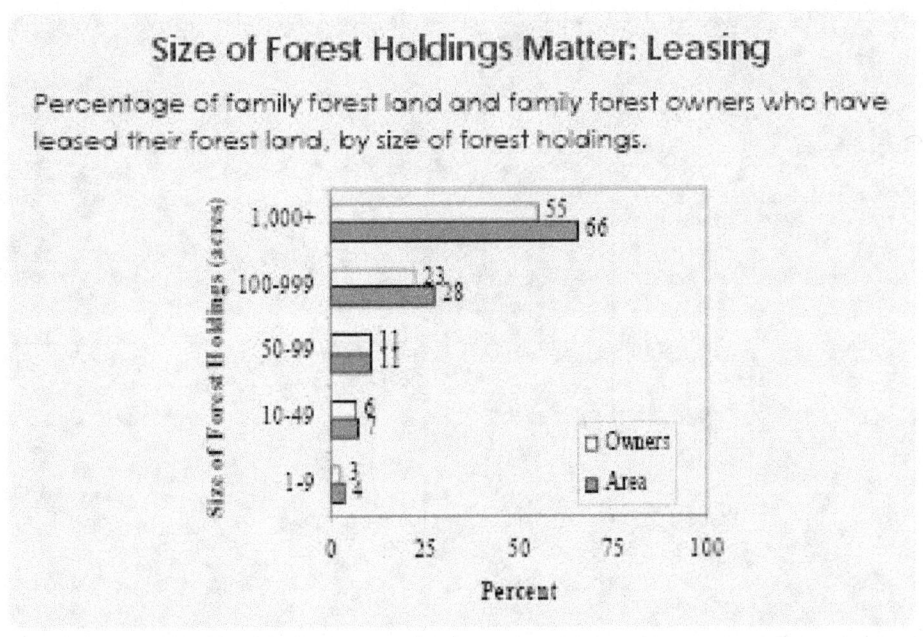

Size of Forest Holdings Matter: Leasing

Percentage of family forest land and family forest owners who have leased their forest land, by size of forest holdings.

Participation in Cost-share, Easements, and Sustainable Forest Certification Programs

Most family forest owners have not participated in cost-share programs, have not participated in a forest certification program, nor do they have an easement on their land (Fig. 13). Cost-share programs may be sponsored by federal or state agencies or private groups. Examples of federal programs include the Conservation Reserve Program, the Environmental Quality Incentives Program, the Forest Land Enhancement Program, and the Forest Stewardship Program. Six percent of the family forest owners, who own 21 percent of the family forest land, have participated in at least one cost-share program (Table US-17).

Forest certification programs have been established to recognize and encourage sustainable forest management. Common forest certification systems or programs include American Tree Farm, Green Tag, Forest Stewardship Council, and Sustainable Forestry Initiative. Although 12 percent of the family forest owners, who own 24 percent of the family forest land, have heard of sustainable forest certification, less than 1 percent of the family forest owners, who own 4 percent of the family forest land, are currently enrolled (Table US-16). Another 2 percent of the owners, who control an additional 6 percent of the family forest land, are considering getting their land certified.

Conservation easements are legally binding agreements that restrict land from being used for certain designated purposes; they are voluntarily entered into by the landowner. Although the NWOS questionnaire provided a definition of conservation easements (Butler et al. 2005), it failed to mention the voluntary nature of the agreements and many respondents included rights-of-way and other easements in their responses. This shortcoming will be rectified in future iterations of the NWOS. Statistics reported here include only owners who indicated that land use conversion is restricted, but these numbers are still high compared to other sources (e.g., Land Trust Alliance 2006). Consequently, the easements reported here should be interpreted as including conservation easements as well as all other easements. Easements are on some or all of the forest land owned by 2 percent of the family forest owners, who own 4 percent of the family forest land (Table US-15).

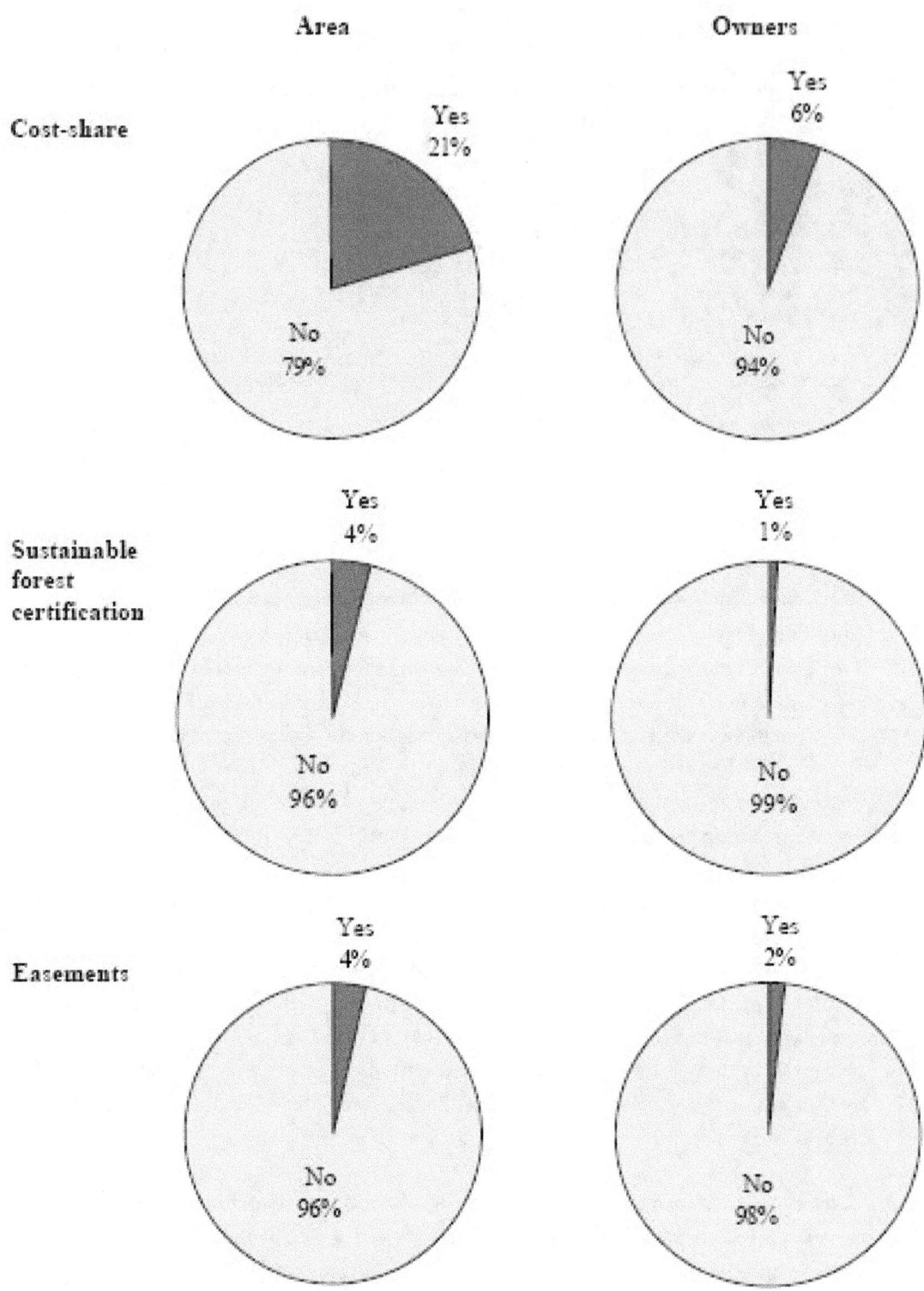

Figure 13.—Participation in cost-share programs, sustainable forest certification, and easements by family forest owners in the United States, 2006.

Size of Forest Holdings Matter: Cost-share, Easements, and Certification

Percentage of family forest land and family forest owners who have participated in (A) cost-share, (B) easement, and (C) certification programs, by size of forest holdings.

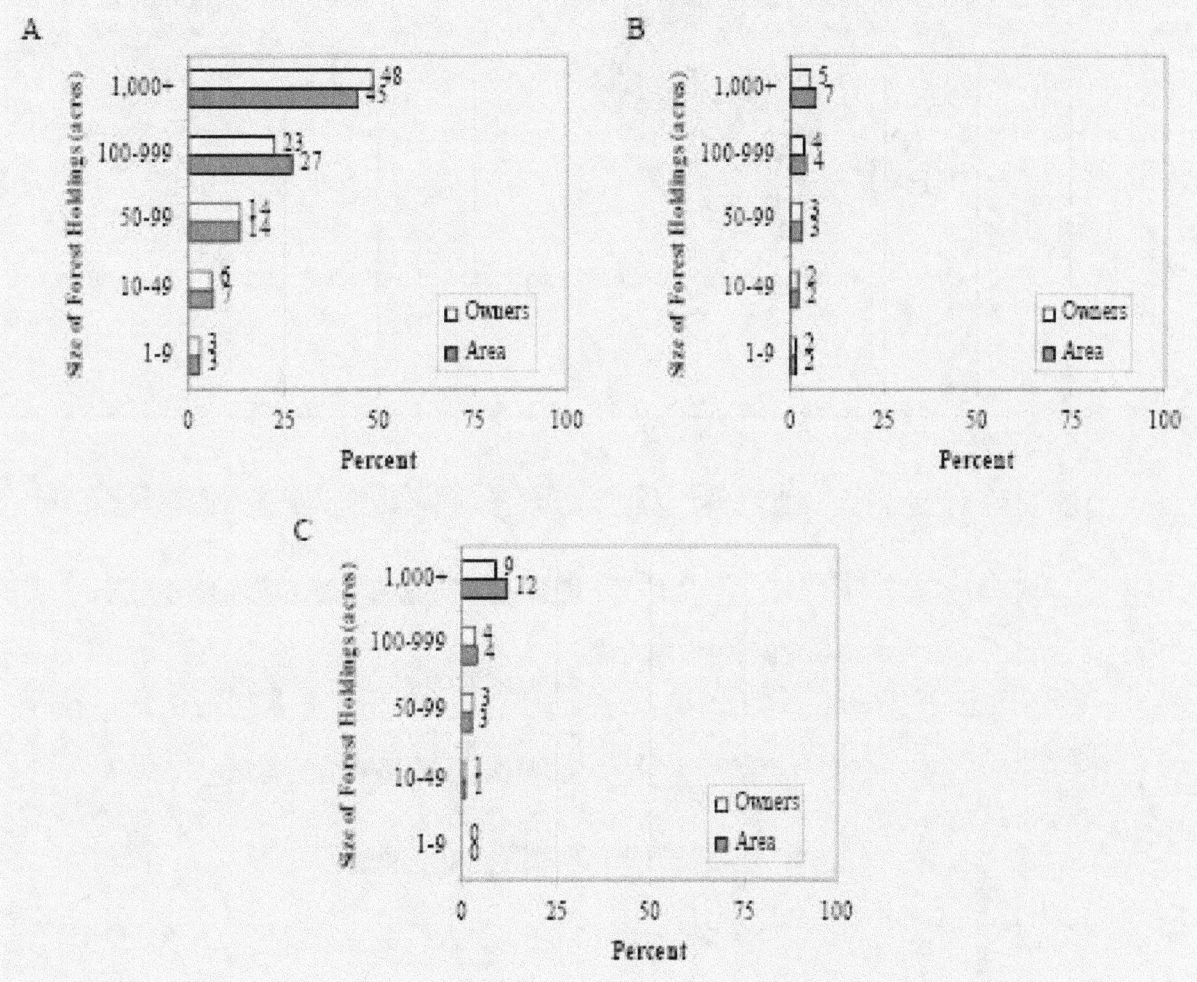

Decisionmakers

Most family forest owners, 92 percent of the family forest owners who own 87 percent of the family forest land, make the management decisions for their forest land themselves (Table US-18). Other family members or a forester are the most common other decisionmakers.

Timber Harvesting and Removals

Although timber production is a primary ownership objective of a minority of the owners (Table US-13), harvesting and removal of trees are still fairly common (Table US-19). About 46 percent of the family forest owners, who own 69 percent of the family forest land, have harvested or removed trees from some or all of their land (Fig. 14). The number of commercial harvests[4] is lower; 27 percent of the family forest owners, who own 58 percent of the family forest land, have commercially harvested trees. The most common reasons for harvesting are related to the maturity, vigor, and health of the forest (Fig. 15, Table US-19).

---

[4]Defined as harvests of sawlogs, pulpwood, and/or veneer logs.

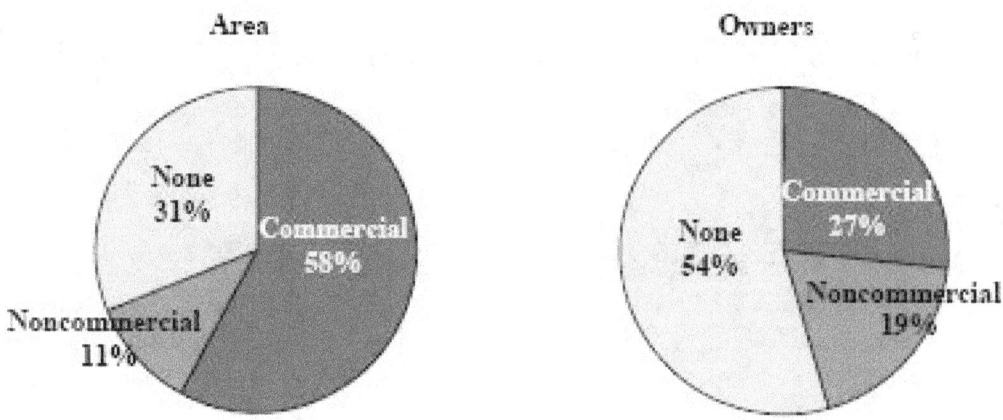

Figure 14.—Commercial and noncommercial harvesting and removal of trees by family forest owners in the United States, 2006.

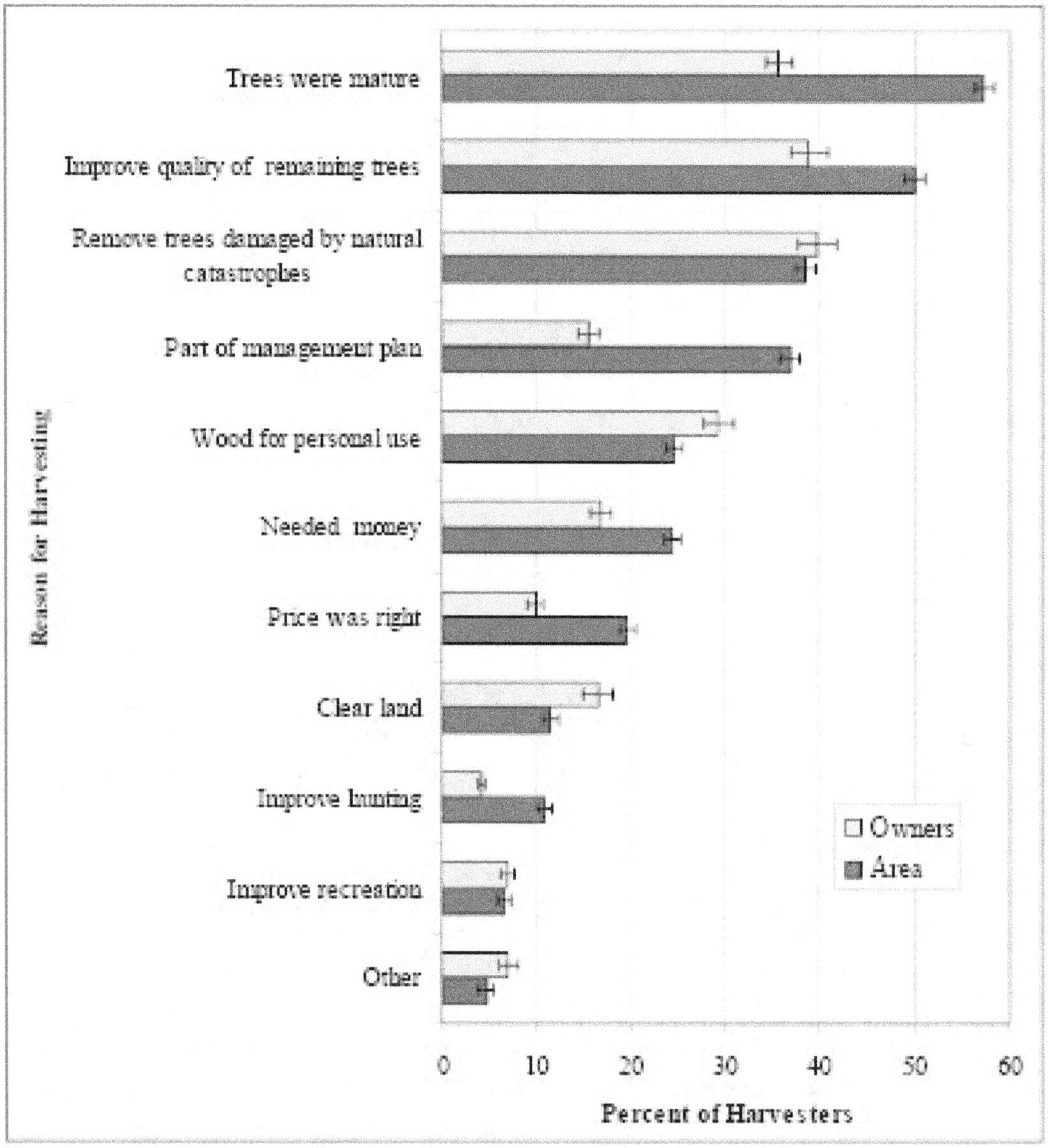

Figure 15.—Reasons for harvesting or removing trees by family forest owners in the United States, 2006. Error bars represent 68 percent confidence intervals.

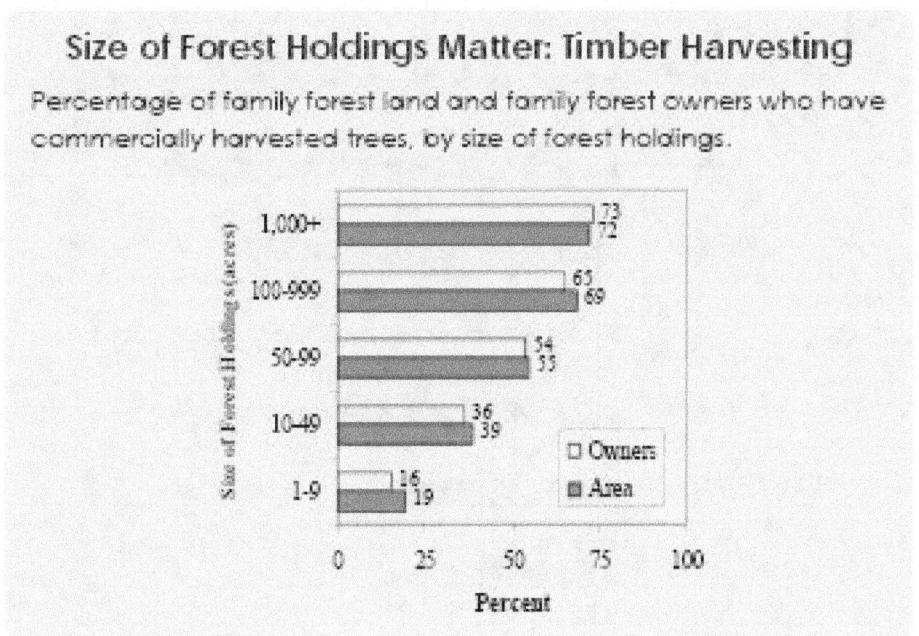

Size of Forest Holdings Matter: Timber Harvesting

Percentage of family forest land and family forest owners who have commercially harvested trees, by size of forest holdings.

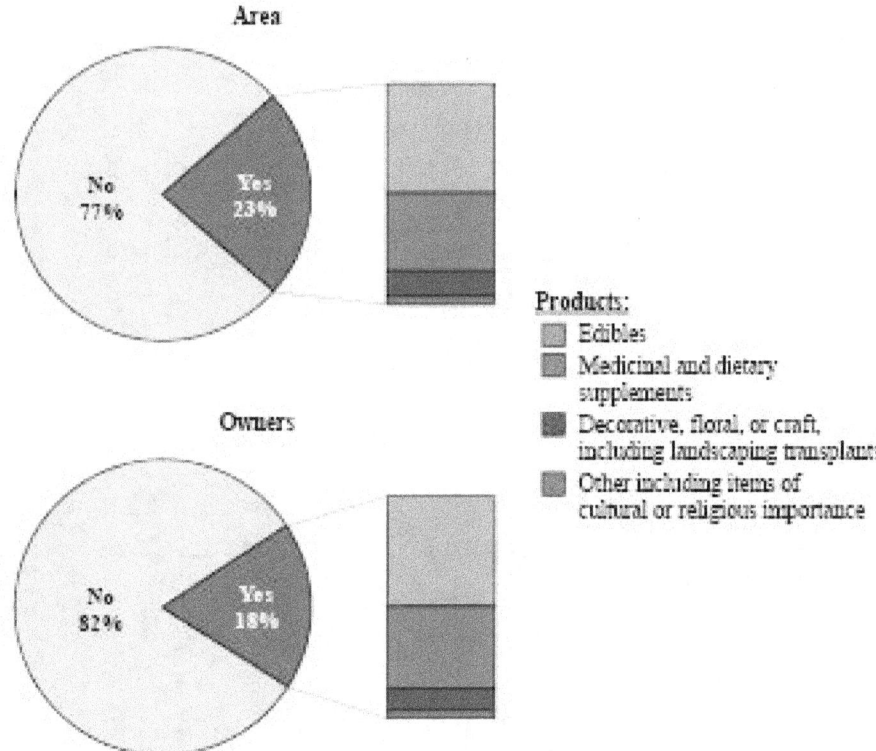

Figure 16.—Collection of nontimber forest products and relative frequency of types of products collected by family forest owners in the United States, 2006.

Nontimber Forest Products

Nontimber forest products (NTFPs), such as mushrooms, pine straw, berries, maple sap, or landscaping transplants, have been harvested or collected on 23 percent of the family forest land owned by 18 percent of the family forest owners (Fig. 16, Table US-20). Most of these NTFPs were collected for personal use (as opposed to being collected for sale) and most were categorized as either edible or decorative.

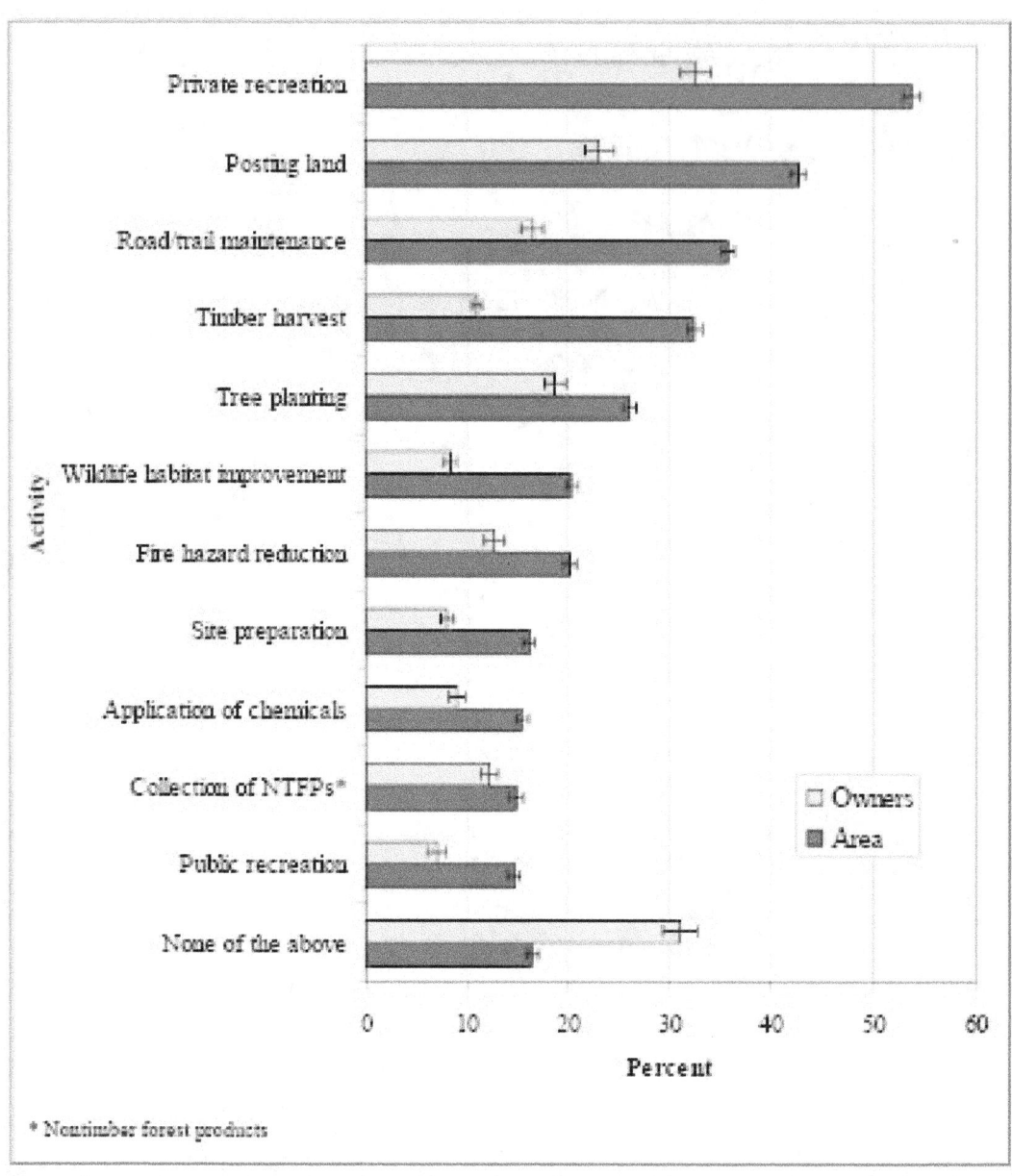

Figure 17.—Forest activities by family forest owners in the United States, 2006. Error bars represent 68 percent confidence intervals.

Other Forest Uses

Other common activities that occur on family forest lands include: recreation, road/trail maintenance, and tree planting (Fig. 17, Table US-22). Recreation is primarily by the landowner, their family, and friends and many landowners post their land to discourage others from accessing it. Seven percent of the family forest owners, who own 15 percent of the family forest land, allow the general public to recreate on their land.

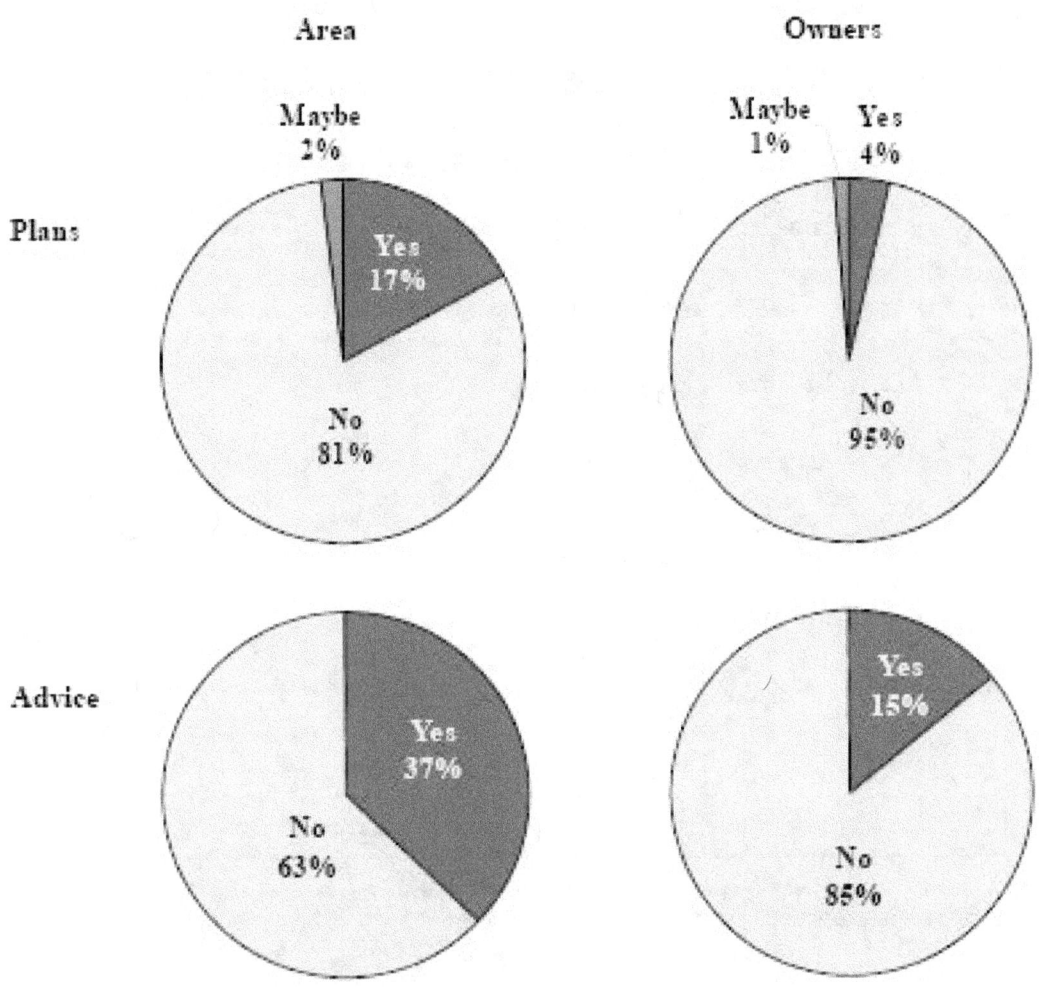

Figure 18.—Management plans and advice received by family forest owners in the United States, 2006.

Forest Management Plans and Advice

Four percent of the family owners, who own 17 percent of the family forest land, report having a written forest management plan (Fig. 18, Table US-21). When asked if they received advice about their forest land, these percentages increase substantially, but still well below half answered affirmatively; 14 percent of the family forest owners, who own 37 percent of the family forest land, received advice about their forest land (Table US-23). The most common sources of advice are state forestry agencies and private consultants (Fig. 19).

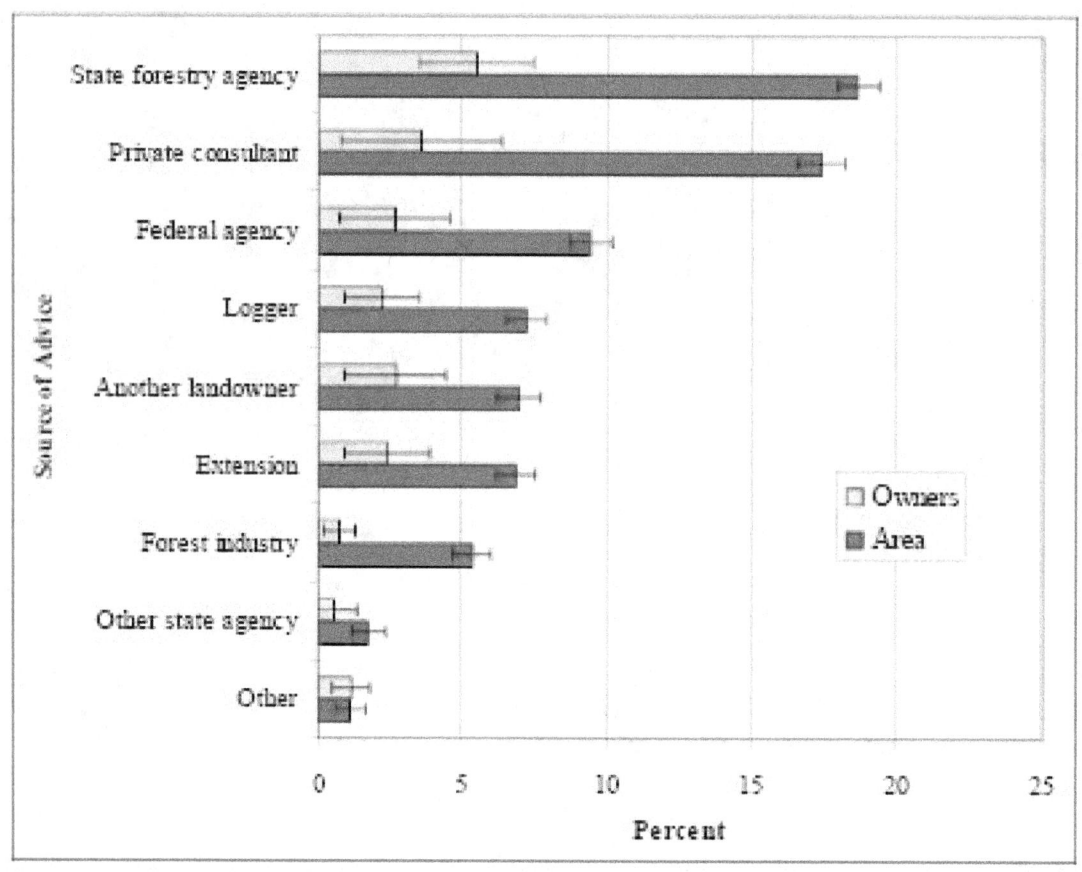

Figure 19.—Sources of forest management advice for family forest owners in the United States, 2006. Error bars represent 68 percent confidence intervals.

Size of Forest Holdings Matter: Management Plans and Advice

Percentage of family forest land and family forest owners who have (A) written forest management plans, and (B) received forest management advice, by size of forest holdings.

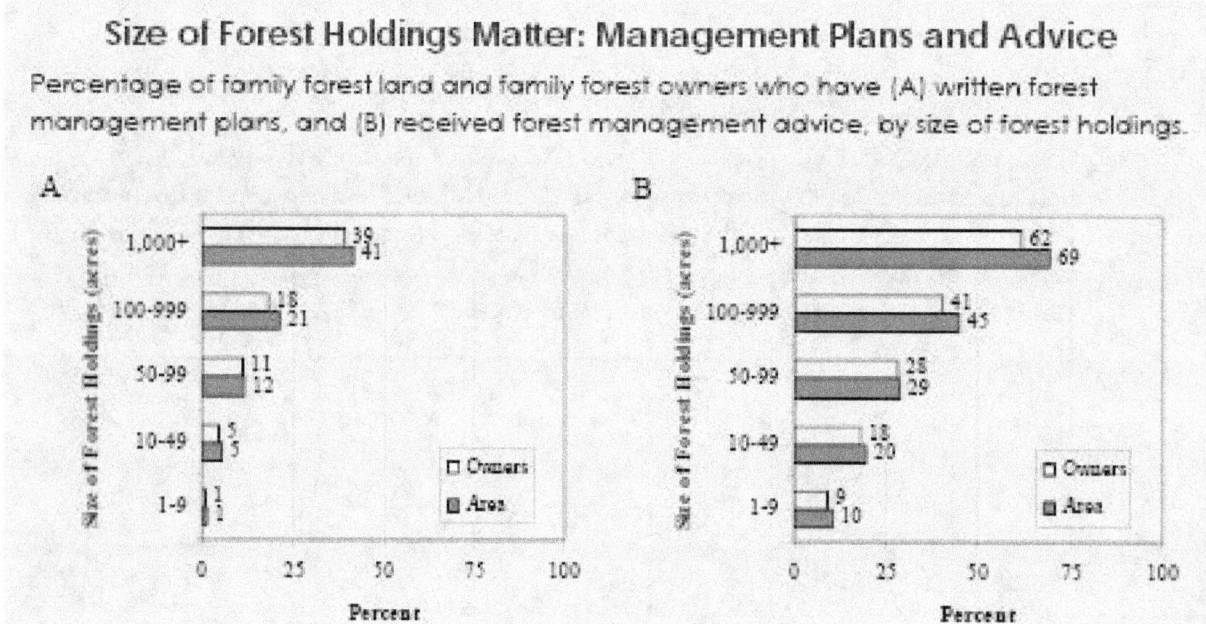

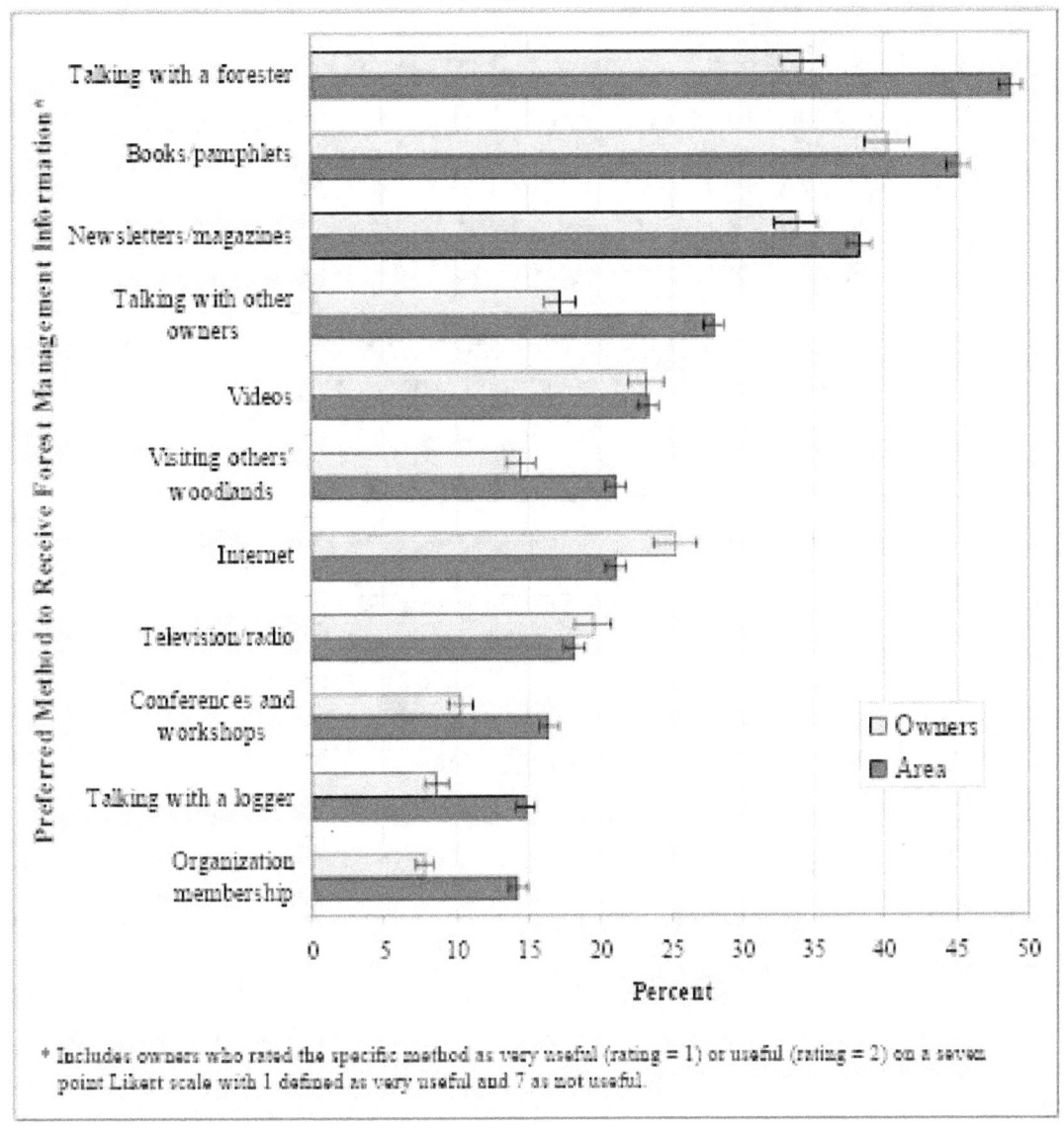

Figure 20.—Preferred methods to receive information about forest management for family forest owners in the United States, 2006. Error bars represent 68 percent confidence intervals.

Preferred Methods for Receiving Forest Management Information

Talking with a forester, publications, and newsletters were rated as useful or very useful[5] methods for obtaining forest management information by at least one-third of the owners, who own at least one-third of the family forest land (Fig. 20, Table US-24). The next tier of preferred methods to receive information includes talking with other owners, videos, visiting other owners' forests, and the Internet. It is clear that there is no single preference for all owners and many owners are interested in multiple methods.

---

[5] Includes owners who rated the specific methods as very useful (rating = 1) or useful (rating = 2) on a seven point Likert scale with 1 defined as very useful and 7 as not useful.

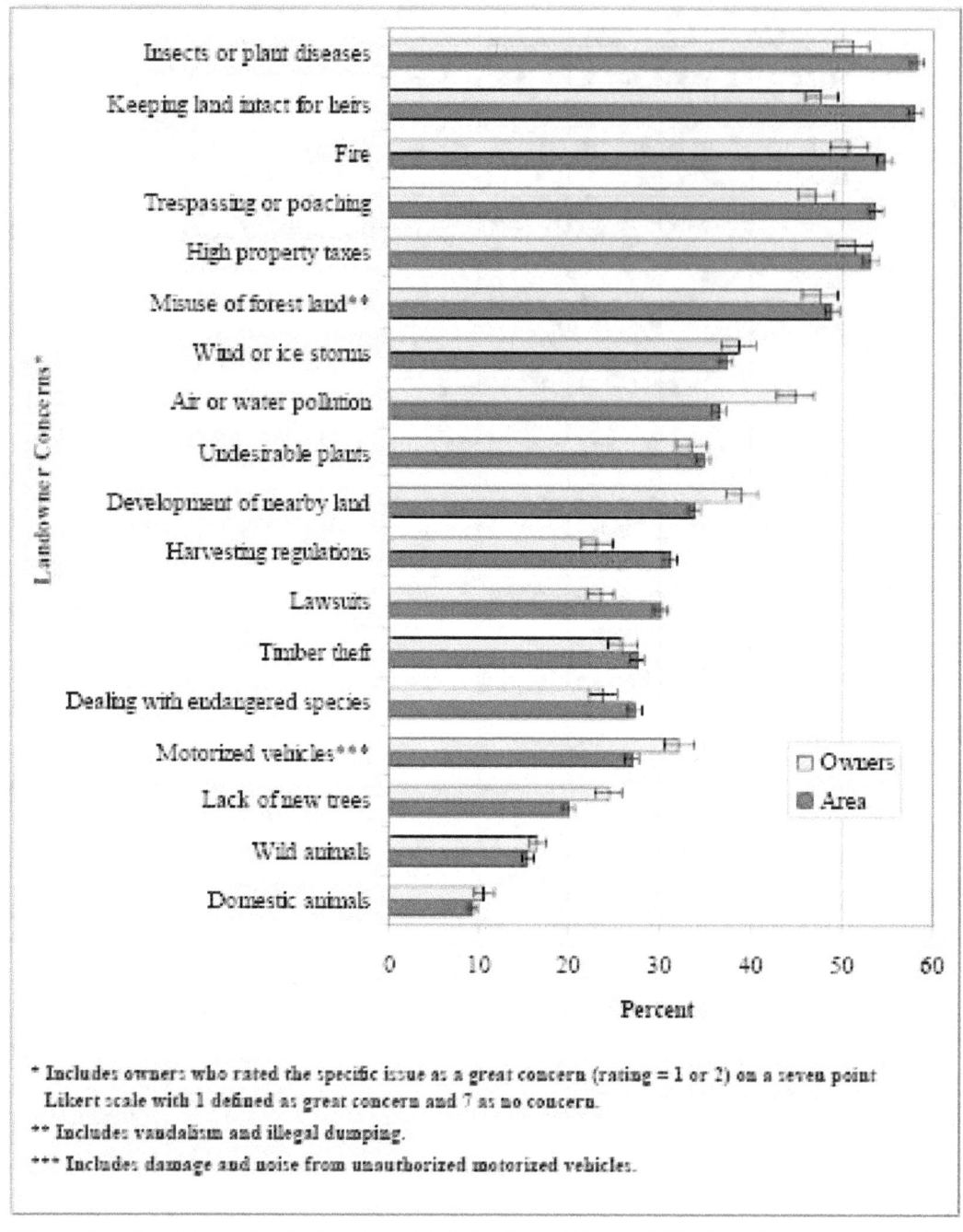

Figure 21.—Concerns of family forest owners in the United States, 2006. Error bars represent 68 percent confidence intervals.

Landowners' Concerns

Many family forest owners are concerned that external forces will adversely affect their forests and their ability to use their forests as they desire. The most commonly rated major concerns[6] are keeping land intact for their heirs, insects and plant diseases, fire, trespassing, and property taxes (Fig. 21, Tables US-25 and US-26). Other relatively common concerns are misuse of the

---

[6]Includes owners who rated the specific issue as a great concern (rating = 1 or 2) on a seven point Likert scale with 1 defined as great concern and 7 as no concern.

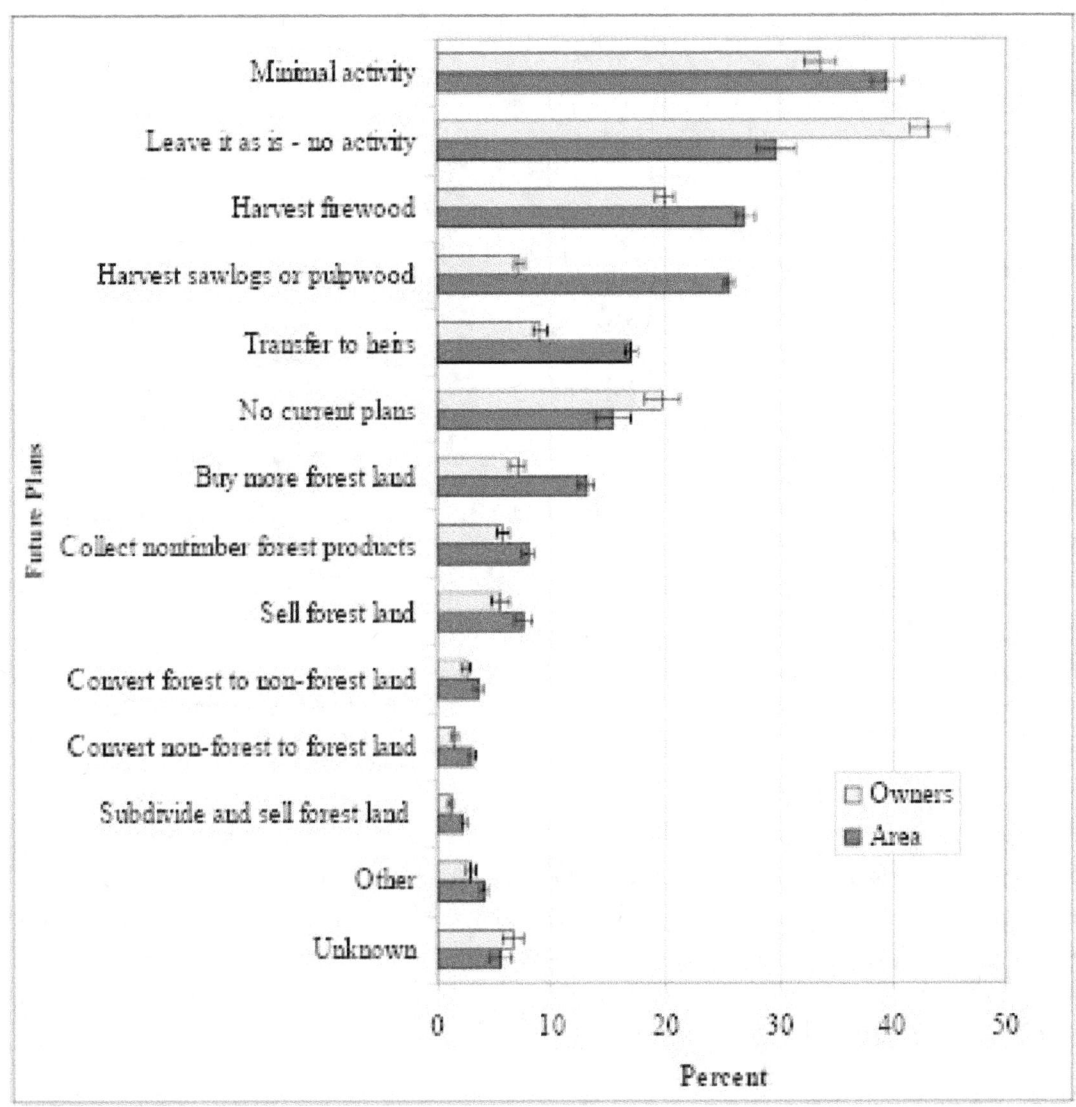

Figure 22.—Future (next 5 years) plans of family forest owners in the United States, 2006. Error bars represent 68 percent confidence intervals.

land (e.g., illegal dumping), damage from storms, air and water pollution, undesirable plants, development of nearby lands, harvesting regulations, and lawsuits.

Future Plans

Most family forest owners plan few activities for their forest land in the next 5 years (Fig. 22, Table US-27). Of those who do intend to actively do something with their land, harvesting sawlogs or pulpwood and harvesting firewood are the most commonly planned activities. There is also a sizable amount of land that is owned by people who plan to sell or transfer some or all of their forest land in the next 5 years (55 million acres ± 3 percent; 14 percent of the family forest owners who own 23 percent of the family forest land[7]).

---

[7]These numbers are slightly lower than those computed by simply combining the "sell" and "transfer" categories because the categories are not exclusive —some owners plan to do both.

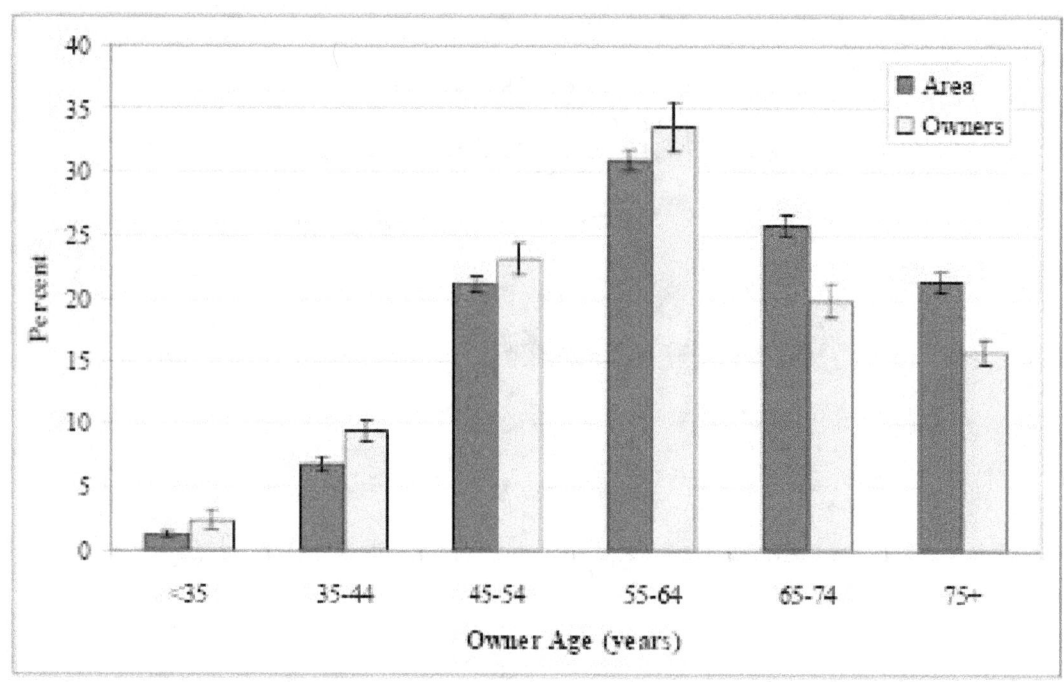

Figure 23.—Age of family forest owners in the United States, 2006. Error bars represent 68 percent confidence intervals.

Demographics

Demographic information was collected for the self-proclaimed, primary decisionmaker for the forest land. In many circumstances, the forest land is jointly owned, but the primary decisionmaker was asked to complete the questionnaire. This information is utilized to help design effective communication tools, to help ensure public forestry programs comply with anti-discrimination policies, and other uses.

Forty-nine percent of the family forest owners, who own 52 percent of the family forest land, are retirees (Table US-28). Of those who are still working, the most common occupation categories are professionals (e.g., engineers and accountants), officials and managers (e.g., CEOs and administrators), and craft workers (e.g., carpenters and mechanics). An additional 5 percent of the owners, who own 9 percent of the family forest land, reported their occupation as a farmer. Classification of the owners' occupations is based on the U.S. Office of Management and Budget's Standard Occupational Classification Manual (2000) using the U.S. Census Bureau's collapsing rules (U.S. Census Bureau 2000).

The high percentage of retirees is correlated with the advanced age of many of the family forest owners. Fifteen percent of the owners, who own 20 percent of the family forest land, are 75 years or older (Fig. 23, Table US-29). An additional 19 percent of the owners, who own an additional 24 percent of the family forest land, are between the ages of 65 and 74. Looking at people in the general population who are 25 years or older, 10 percent of them are between 65 and 74 years of age and 9 percent are 75 years or older (Fig. 24A)

Compared to the general public (U.S. Census Bureau 2001a, 2001b), family forest owners' education and income levels are relatively high (Fig. 24B and 24C). Thirty-one percent of

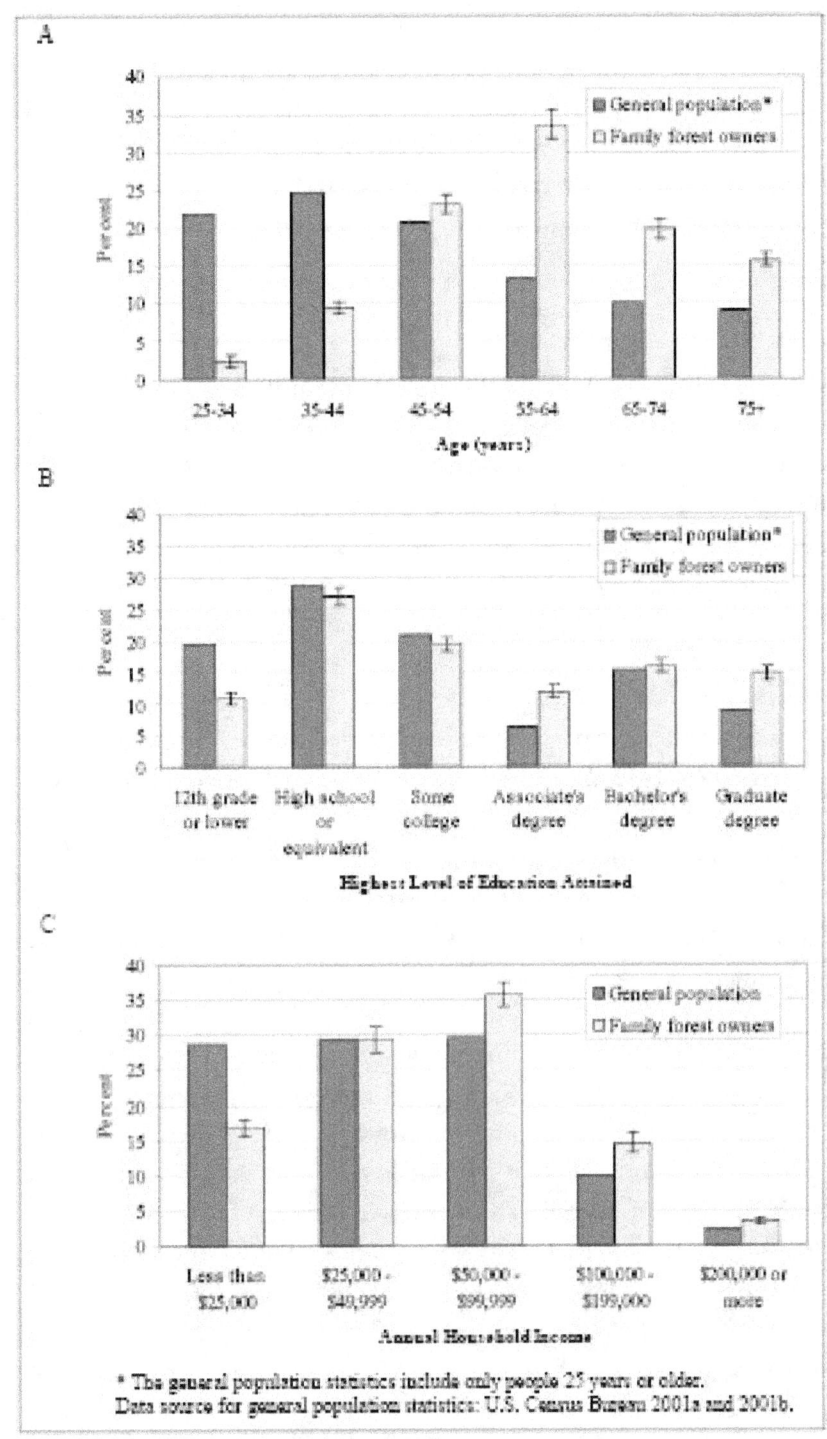

Figure 24.—Comparison of (A) age, (B) education, and (C) annual household income between family forest owners and the general population. Error bars represent 68 percent confidence intervals.

the owners, who own 41 percent of the family forest land, have at least a bachelor's degree compared to 24 percent of the general population[8] (Table US-30). Eighteen percent of the family owners, who own 27 percent of the family forest land, have annual household incomes of at least $100,000 compared to 12 percent of the general population (Table US-31).

---

[8] Including only owners who are 25 years or older.

Demographically, family forest owners are relatively homogeneous. Most of the primary decisionmakers are white males (Tables US-32 and US-33); 72 percent of the family forest owners, who own 78 percent of the family forest land, are male and 95 percent of the family forest owners, who own 96 percent of the family forest land, are white. About 16 percent of the owners, who own 17 percent of the family forest land, have a physical disability (Table US-34). Seven percent of the family forest owners, who own 8 percent of the family forest land, have a vision or hearing impediment.

CONCLUSIONS

America's family forest owners are diverse, dynamic, and numerous. There are 10.4 million of them (± 3 percent) who collectively own 264 million acres of forest land (± 0.4 percent) or 35 percent of the forests in the United States. Collectively, they own a plurality of the forest land and are thus pivotal to achieving broad-scale, sustainable forest management goals. Numerous surveys and other research initiatives have focused on family forest owners (see review in Hodgdon and Tyrrell 2003), but the NWOS is the only national-level survey of family forest owners that is scientifically based and has been completed for multiple iterations (i.e., 1993 and 2006).

As shown in Figure 8 and the "Size of Forest Holdings Matter" sidebars, the size of forest holdings is an important determinant, or at least correlate, with many of the attributes of family forest owners. It is positively correlated with having a written forest management plan, having received forest management advice, and conducting commercial timber harvests. If the size of forest holdings continue to decrease, as many experts expect it to do (e.g., Sampson and DeCoster 2000, Best and Wayburn 2001), the overall attitudes and behaviors of family forest owners will continue to change.

Most family forest owners are interested in the amenities, such as beauty, scenery, and privacy, that their forests provide. Given the predicted decrease in size of forest holdings and other societal factors (e.g., increasing incomes) these amenities are likely to increase in importance. This has important implications for how the land is viewed by the owners and subsequently managed. Timber production is not a primary objective of most family forest owners, but timber harvesting is a common activity. How can forestry professionals bring forest management to the forefront of family forest owners' minds and help ensure that owners are meeting their needs and sound forest management is being conducted? A better understanding of owners' needs and concerns is a first step. The next step is to turn this knowledge into actionable plans (e.g., Butler et al. 2007).

Family forest ownership patterns will continue to change as land passes from one generation to the next, within families or otherwise. Twenty-three percent of the family forest land is owned by people who intend to sell or transfer their land soon. This is related to the fact that 20 percent of the family forest land is owned by people who are 75 years or older. The magnitude of changes in the attitudes and behaviors between the current and future owners will be a function of, among other things, the background, objectives, and circumstances of the new owners and the characteristics of their land. For example, will the new owners be more or less likely to have rural backgrounds, will they be more or less likely to be absentee owners, will they own smaller or larger parcels of forest land, will they be more or less interested in earning money from their land and if they are, from what sources, timber or land sales? These and many other unanswered questions will shape the future of America's family forest owners and America's forest lands.

The NWOS findings have important implications for organizations that rely on, provide services to, or otherwise interact with family forest owners. Increased understanding of family forest owners will lead to better forest policies, more effective outreach campaigns, services and programs better suited to meet owners' needs, and a heightened awareness of the importance of family forest owners. Through continued implementation of the NWOS and related research, we hope to monitor trends and further refine our understanding of America's family forest owners.

ACKNOWLEDGMENTS

I would like to thank the thousands of forest owners who graciously participated in this survey. Without the hard work and foresight of my predecessor, Tom Birch, and former colleague, Earl Leatherberry, the NWOS would not be what it is today. Mark Brown and John Winborne provided critical assistance in data preparation and processing. My fellow FIA employees, from the field crews who collected the names and addresses, to the people in the office who compiled the lists and numbers, are the unsung backbone of the NWOS. The generous support of the U.S. Forest Service, State and Private Forestry, Cooperative Forestry program has been essential to the success of the NWOS. The guidance and support of the NWOS steering committee and the community of people interested in private forest ownership issues have greatly improved the NWOS. I am very grateful for the review comments provided by Mark Brown, Mark Buccowich, Sally Campbell, Karl Dalla Rosa, Bill Hubbard, and others.

LITERATURE CITED

Azuma, D.L.; Hiserote, B.A.; Dunham, P.A. 2005. The western juniper resource of eastern Oregon, 1999. Resour. Bull. PNW-249. Portland, OR: U.S. Department of Agriculture, Forest Service, Pacific Northwest Research Station. 18 p.

Bechtold, W.A.; Patterson, P.L. 2005. The enhanced Forest Inventory and Analysis program— national sampling design and estimation procedures. Gen. Tech. Rep. SRS-80. Asheville, NC: U.S. Department of Agriculture, Forest Service, Southern Research Station. 85 p.

Best, C.; Wayburn, L.A. 2001. America's private forests: status and stewardship. Washington, DC: Island Press. 268 p.

Birch, T.W. 1996a. Private forest-land owners of the United States, 1994. Resour. Bull. NE-134. Radnor, PA: U.S. Department of Agriculture, Forest Service, Northeastern Forest Experiment Station. 183 p.

Birch, T.W. 1996b. Private forest-land owners of the Northern United States, 1994. Resour. Bull. NE-136. Radnor, PA: U.S. Department of Agriculture, Forest Service, Northeastern Forest Experiment Station. 293 p.

Birch, T.W. 1996c. Private forest-land owners of the Southern United States, 1994. Resour. Bull. NE-138. Radnor, PA: U.S. Department of Agriculture, Forest Service, Northeastern Forest Experiment Station. 195 p.

Birch, T.W. 1996d. Private forest-land owners of the Western United States, 1994. Resour. Bull. NE-137. Radnor, PA: U.S. Department of Agriculture, Forest Service, Northeastern Forest Experiment Station. 249 p.

Birch, T.W.; Lewis, D.G.; Kaiser, H.F. 1982. The private forest-land owners of the United States. Resour. Bull. WO-1. Washington, DC: U.S. Department of Agriculture, Forest Service. 64 p.

Butler, B.J.; Leatherberry, E.C.; Williams, M.S. 2005. Design, implementation, and analysis methods for the National Woodland Owner Survey. Gen. Tech. Rep. NE-336. Newtown Square, PA: U.S. Department of Agriculture, Forest Service, Northeastern Research Station. 43 p.

Butler, B.J.; Tyrrell, M.; Feinberg, G.; et al. 2007. Understanding and reaching family forest owners: lessons from social marketing research. Journal of Forestry. 105(7): 348-357.

Campbell, S.; van Hees, W.W.S.; Mead, B. 2004. Southeast Alaska forests: inventory highlights. Gen. Tech. Rep. PNW-609. Portland, OR: U.S. Department of Agriculture, Forest Service, Pacific Northwest Research Station. 20 p.

Campbell, S.; van Hees, W.W.S.; Mead, B. 2005. South-central Alaska forests: inventory highlights. Gen. Tech. Rep. PNW-652. Portland, OR: U.S. Department of Agriculture, Forest Service, Pacific Northwest Research Station. 28 p.

Crocker, S.J.; Moser, W.K.; Brand, G.J.; et al. 2006. Iowa's forest resources in 2004. Resour. Bull. NC-263. St. Paul, MN: U.S. Department of Agriculture, Forest Service, North Central Research Station. 34 p.

Dillman, D.A. 2001. Mail and internet surveys: the tailored design method. New York: Wiley. 464 p.

Hodgdon, B.; Tyrrell, M. 2003. Literature review: an annotated bibliography on family forest owners. GISF Research Paper 002. New Haven, CT: Yale University, School of Forestry and Environmental Studies, Global Institute of Sustainable Forestry. 17 p.

Josephson, H.R.; McGuire, J.R. 1958. Ownership of forest land and timber. In: Timber resources for America's future. For. Res. Rep. No. 14. Washington, DC: U.S. Department of Agriculture, Forest Service. 289-321.

Land Trust Alliance. 2006. 2005 National land trust census report. Washington, DC. 22 p. http://www.lta.org/census/. (accessed 30 November 2007).

Powell, D.S.; Faulkner, J.L.; Darr, D.R.; Zhu, Z.; MacCleery, D.W. 1993. Forest resources of the United States, 1992. Gen. Tech. Rep. RM-234. Fort Collins, CO: U.S. Department of Agriculture, Forest Service, Rocky Mountain Forest and Range Experiment Station. 132 p.

Sampson, R.N.; DeCoster, L. 2000. Forest fragmentation: implications for sustainable private forests. Journal of Forestry. 98(3): 4-8.

Smith, W.B.; Miles, P.D.; Hoppus, M.; et al. In press. Forest resources of the United States, 2007. U.S. Department of Agriculture, Forest Service.

Smith, W.B.; Miles, P.D.; Vissage, J.S.; et al. 2004. Forest resources of the United States, 2002. Gen. Tech. Rep. NC-241. St. Paul, MN: U.S. Department of Agriculture, Forest Service, North Central Research Station. 137 p.

U.S. Census Bureau. 2000. Census 2000 special EEO tabulation: occupational crosswalk to EEO occupational groups and EEO-1 job categories. Washington, DC: U.S. Department of Commerce, Census Bureau. 16 p. http://www.census.gov/hhes/www/eeoindex/jobgroups.pdf. (accessed 9 July 2007).

U.S. Census Bureau. 2001a. Census 2000 summary file 1 for the United States. Washington, DC: U.S. Department of Commerce, Census Bureau. http://www.census.gov/main/www/cen2000.html. (accessed 7 November 2007).

U.S. Census Bureau. 2001b. Census 2000 summary file 3 for the United States. Washington, DC: U.S. Department of Commerce, Census Bureau. http://www.census.gov/main/www/cen2000.html. (accessed 7 November 2007).

U.S. Office of Management and Budget, National Technical Information Service. 2000. Standard occupational classification manual. Washington, DC: U.S. Office of Management and Budget, National Technical Information Service. 257 p.

USDA Forest Service, Forest Inventory and Analysis. 2005. Forest Inventory and Analysis: National core field guide. Volume I: field data collection procedures for phase 2 plots. Version 3.0. Washington, DC: U.S. Department of Agriculture, Forest Service. 203 p. http://www.fia.fs.fed.us/library/field-guides-methods-proc/docs/2006/core_ver_3-0_10_2005.pdf. (accessed 10 July 2007).

USDA National Agricultural Statistics Service. 2004. 2002 Census of Agriculture, United States summary and State data, Volume 1. AC-02-A-51. Washington, DC: U.S. Department of Agriculture, National Agricultural Statistics Service. 657 p. http://www.nass.usda.gov/census/census02/volume1/USVolume104.pdf. (accessed 30 November 2007).

APPENDIX I: DATA AND METHODS

Full details of the design, implementation, estimation, and analysis of the NWOS are available in Butler et al. (2005), which is included on the CD in the back of this publication. Presented here is a synopsis of that publication and descriptions of how special circumstances were handled.

The NWOS is conducted by the U.S. Forest Service, FIA program to increase our understanding of:

- Who owns the forests of the United States
- Why they own them
- How they use them
- What they intend to do with them

On an annual basis, the NWOS uses an area-based sampling frame to contact approximately 6,000 private forest owners from across the United States. First, a grid is established with the cell size commensurate with the sampling intensity for the given state. Within each cell, a point is randomly selected. Remote sensing and site visits are used to determine which points are forested. The owner of record is collected from public tax records for all forested plots. The methods prescribed by Dillman (2001) are used to contact the private owners and persuade them to complete the self-administered mail questionnaires. Between 2002 and 2006, 15,440 family forest owners participated in the NWOS (Table A). The overall cooperation rate was 51.3 percent.

Forest land refers to land at least 1 acre in size and "at least 10 percent stocked by forest trees of any size, including land that formerly had such tree cover and that will be naturally or artificially regenerated" (Smith et al. 2004). Family forests are defined as forest land owned by families, individuals, trusts, estates, family partnerships, and unincorporated groups of individuals. This category is synonymous with the "individual" owner class used by the FIA forest inventory (USDA For. Serv. 2005) and the 1993 NWOS (Birch 1996a). Nonindustrial private forests (NIPF) are forests owned by private families, individuals, corporations, or other groups that neither own nor operate a primary wood processing facility; family forests are a subset of nonindustrial private forests. This is synonymous with the NIPF definition used by the FIA forest inventory and Forest Resources of the United States, 2002 (Smith et al. 2004).

Forest land area by ownership group and associated variances were derived from the database assembled for the Renewable Resources Planning Act Assessment report (i.e., Smith et al., in press). These data come from the most recently completed state-level FIA forest surveys. Areas were calculated by summing the area expansion factors that were calculated using the methods described in Bechtold and Patterson (2005). Variances were calculated using (nonstratified) simple random sampling algorithms adapted from Bechtold and Patterson (2005). To avoid pseudo-replication, only plot center (condition number one) was used in the variance calculations.

Estimates were made for each of the estimation units depicted in Figure 25. These sampling units are a superset of the FIA forest survey units (USDA For. Serv. 2005). In general, forest survey unit numbers do not match the NWOS estimation unit numbers. A minimum of

Figure 25.—Estimation units used to calculate National Woodland Owner Survey results. Estimation units do not cross state boundaries.

25 responses from family forest owners were required for each sampling unit. When this requirement was not met, adjacent survey units within a state were collapsed. State-level estimates were made by summing the sub-state level estimates.

Area and owner estimates were made separately. Area estimates were made using simple random sample estimators (Butler et al. 2005). To adjust for unequal inclusion probabilities, probability proportional to size estimators were used to calculate owner estimates (Butler et al. 2005). The unequal inclusion probabilities arise because we use an area-based sampling frame and therefore owners with larger parcels have a higher probability of being included than owners with smaller parcels.

Differences between sample estimates and true population values can arise due to sampling error, coverage error, measurement error, and nonresponse error (Dillman 2001). Since we used a random sample design, coverage errors are not an issue. Measurement errors are the result of poor questions. To assure good wording, the survey instrument was pretested and a national committee of experts reviewed it.

Tests were performed to identify potential nonresponse errors. Size of forest holdings is an important variable and is integral for making estimates of number of owners (see Statistical Estimation Procedures in Butler et al. 2005). Hence, this variable was the principal variable used to test for nonresponse bias. Tests were conducted using ancillary data (e.g., size of parcels from tax records) and by segregating data by various spatial units (to test for differences along the urban-rural continuum). No statistically significant biases were detected.

Sampling errors are the result of not all members of a population being included in a survey. As the number of participants approaches the number in the population, the sampling error will approach zero. Sampling errors are reported for estimates in percentage terms. Sampling errors should always be considered when looking at specific estimates. Estimates with sampling errors greater than or equal to 50 percent should be used very cautiously. All estimates with sampling errors greater than or equal to 25 percent should be used with caution. Estimates can be improved (i.e., sampling errors reduced) by increasing the sampling intensity and/or increasing the response rate.

No NWOS data were collected for interior Alaska, Hawaii, Nevada, western Oklahoma, or western Texas between 2002 and 2006. In the national summary tables (i.e., Tables B to E), forest area statistics were taken from the 2007 RPA data (Smith et al., in press) and ownership data were taken from the 1993 ownership survey (Birch 1996c, 1996d). As noted in the footnotes of the tables, interior Alaska, Hawaii, Nevada, western Oklahoma, and western Texas are excluded from all other tables. The coastal area of Alaska that is included here is defined as the southeast and south-central portions of Alaska as defined in Campbell et al. (2004) and Campbell et al. (2005) and depicted in Figure 2.

INDEX OF TABLES

National, Regional, and State Tables

The NWOS results are summarized in separate sets of tables for the United States, regions, and states (Fig. 2). These tables are based on data collected between 2002 and 2006. The U.S. tables are included in the printed portion of this report (labeled A through E and US-1 through -34) and all of the tables are included on the accompanying CD. The tables are numbered the same with identifiers prior to the numbers used to identify the specific table set. The identifiers are US for the national tables, NORTH, SOUTH, ROCKY, or PACIFIC for the regional tables, and the two-letter state abbreviations for the state tables. The tables are:

Table US-8.—Area and number of family forests in the United States by type and source of forest land acquisition, 2006

Table US-9.—Area and number of family forests in the United States by ownership tenure, 2006

Table US-10.—Area and number of family forests in the United States by frequency and recipient of forest land transfers, 2006

Table US-11.—Area and number of family forests in the United States by form of ownership, 2006

Table US-12.—Area and number of family forests in the United States that are associated with owners' farms, primary homes, and vacation homes, 2006

Table US-13.—Area and number of family forests in the United States by reason for owning forest land, 2006. Numbers include landowners who ranked each objective as very important (1) or important (2) on a seven-point Likert scale.

Table US-14.—Area and number of family forests in the United States by lease status, 2006

Table US-15.—Area and number of family forests in the United States by status of easements that restrict land use conversions, 2006

Table US-16.—Area and number of family forests in the United States by knowledge of and participation in sustainable forest certification programs, 2006

Table US-17.—Area and number of family forests in the United States by participation in cost-share programs, 2006

Table US-18.—Area and number of family forests in the United States by primary forest management decisionmaker, 2006

Table US-19.—Area and number of family forests in the United States by timber harvesting activities and reasons, 2006

Table US-20.—Area and number of family forests in the United States by activities related to nontimber forest products (NTFPs), 2006

Table US-21.—Area and number of family forests in the United States by management plan status, 2006

Table US-22.—Area and number of family forests in the United States by recent (past 5 years) forestry activity, 2006

Table US-23.—Area and number of family forests in the United States by advice received and advice source, 2006

Table US-24.—Area and number of family forests in the United States by preferred methods to receive forest management information, 2006. Numbers include landowners who ranked each method as very useful (1) or useful (2) on a seven-point Likert scale.

Table US-25.—Area and number of family forests in the United States by landowners' sociopolitical concerns, 2006. Numbers include landowners who ranked each issue as a very important (1) or important (2) concern on a seven-point Likert scale.

Table US-26.—Area and number of family forests in the United States by landowners' forest health concerns, 2006. Numbers include landowners who ranked each issue as a very important (1) or important (2) concern on a seven-point Likert scale.

Table US-27.—Area and number of family forests in the United States by landowners' future (next 5 years) plans for their forest land, 2006

Table US-28.—Area and number of family forests in the United States by primary occupation of the primary decisionmaker, 2006

Table US-29.—Area and number of family forests in the United States by age of the primary decisionmaker, 2006

Table US-30.—Area and number of family forests in the United States by highest level of formal education of the primary decisionmaker, 2006

Table US-31.—Area and number of family forests in the United States by primary decisionmaker's annual household income, 2006

Table US-32.—Area and number of family forests in the United States by gender of the primary decisionmaker, 2006

Table US-33.—Area and number of family forests in the United States by ethnicity and race of the primary decisionmaker, 2006

Table US-34.—Area and number of family forests in the United States by disability of the primary decisionmaker, 2006

Table A.--Numbers of responses and cooperation rates for family forest owners who participated in the U.S. Forest Services' National Woodland Owner Survey between 2002 and 2006 by region, subregion, and state

Region, subregion, and state	Surveys sent	Number of undeliverables	Number of responses	Cooperation rate
				Percent
North:				
Northeast:				
Connecticut	157	22	77	57.0
Delaware	76	30	19	39.6
Maine	911	122	419	53.1
Maryland	210	36	78	44.6
Massachusetts	203	29	82	47.1
New Hampshire	254	52	119	58.9
New Jersey	107	24	35	42.2
New York	1,313	261	424	40.3
Pennsylvania	2,876	169	1,205	44.5
Rhode Island	74	8	33	50.0
Vermont	317	73	147	60.2
West Virginia	650	107	245	45.1
Northeast total:	7,152	933	2,883	46.4
North Central:				
Illinois	641	51	327	55.4
Indiana	533	57	270	56.7
Iowa	392	46	206	59.5
Michigan	3,683	414	2,028	62.0
Minnesota	1,421	268	743	64.4
Missouri	2,188	285	1,115	58.6
Ohio	495	74	225	53.4
Wisconsin	2,612	390	1,483	66.7
North Central total:	11,965	1,585	6,397	61.6
North total:	19,117	2,518	9,280	55.9
South:				
Southeast:				
Florida	266	40	108	47.8
Georgia	1,714	261	723	49.8
North Carolina	791	59	321	43.9
South Carolina	1,787	211	694	44.0
Virginia	987	76	444	48.7
Southeast total:	5,545	647	2,290	46.8
South Central:				
Alabama	1,848	257	834	52.4
Arkansas	817	161	281	42.8
Kentucky	952	98	375	43.9
Louisiana	372	60	121	38.8
Mississippi	921	341	198	34.1
Oklahoma (east)	263	79	65	35.3
Tennessee	1,585	206	519	37.6
Texas (east)	923	66	386	45.0
South Central total:	7,681	1,268	2,779	43.3
South total:	13,226	1,915	5,069	44.8

Table A. (continued)

Region, subregion, and state	Surveys sent	Number of undeliverables	Number of responses	Cooperation rate
				Percent
Rocky Mountain:				
Great Plains:				
Kansas	366	46	172	53.6
Nebraska	190	23	85	50.9
North Dakota	117	14	41	39.8
South Dakota	79	11	33	48.5
Great Plains total:	752	94	331	50.3
Intermountain:				
Arizona	90	26	27	42.2
Colorado	212	95	65	55.6
Idaho	94	58	18	50.0
Montana	193	82	49	44.1
Nevada	1	0	0	0.0
New Mexico	94	45	20	40.8
Utah	146	28	64	54.2
Wyoming	115	25	42	46.7
Intermountain total:	945	359	285	48.6
Rocky Mountain total:	1,697	453	616	49.5
Pacific Coast:				
Alaska:				
Alaska (coastal):	45	6	20	51.3
Alaska total:	45	6	20	51.3
Pacific Northwest:				
Oregon	272	27	136	55.5
Washington	268	33	130	55.3
Pacific Northwest total:	540	60	266	55.4
Pacific Southwest:				
California	496	77	189	45.1
Hawaii	0	-	-	-
Pacific Southwest total:	496	77	189	45.1
Pacific Coast total:	1,081	143	475	50.6
United States total:	35,121	5,029	15,440	51.3

Table B.--Area of forest land in the United States by ownership category, region, subregion, and state, 2006

Region, subregion, and state	All ownerships		Private					
			Total		Family		Other Private	
	Acres	SE [a]	Acres	SE [a]	Acres	SE [a]	Acres	SE [a]
	Thousands	Percent	Thousands	Percent	Thousands	Percent	Thousands	Percent
North:								
Northeast:								
Connecticut	1,794	6.6	1,383	7.4	898	8.7	485	13.5
Delaware	363	11.2	351	11.6	244	13.7	107	22.0
Maine	17,673	1.3	16,575	1.3	5,727	2.2	10,848	1.7
Maryland	2,566	4.2	1,957	4.8	1,462	5.4	495	10.1
Massachusetts	3,171	4.9	2,179	5.8	1,686	6.2	493	13.8
New Hampshire	4,850	3.4	3,646	3.8	2,358	4.3	1,288	7.3
New Jersey	2,132	4.6	1,322	5.7	805	7.3	517	9.3
New York	18,669	1.7	14,438	1.9	11,252	2.0	3,186	4.7
Pennsylvania	16,577	1.4	11,738	1.7	8,905	1.8	2,832	3.8
Rhode Island	356	10.1	303	10.8	204	12.5	99	20.7
Vermont	4,618	2.6	3,864	2.7	3,109	2.8	755	7.8
West Virginia	12,007	1.5	10,418	1.6	7,174	1.8	3,244	3.1
Northeast total:	84,796	0.7	68,175	0.7	43,825	0.9	24,349	1.3
North Central:								
Illinois	4,525	3.3	3,730	3.6	3,465	3.7	265	14.2
Indiana	4,656	3.0	3,888	3.2	3,471	3.4	417	10.8
Iowa	2,879	4.2	2,552	4.5	2,449	4.5	102	23.1
Michigan	19,545	1.0	12,117	1.2	8,956	1.4	3,161	2.5
Minnesota	16,391	1.1	7,114	1.8	5,390	2.0	1,724	3.7
Missouri	15,076	1.5	12,393	1.6	11,605	1.6	788	7.2
Ohio	7,894	2.5	6,973	2.6	5,796	2.7	1,177	7.1
Wisconsin	16,275	1.0	11,117	1.2	9,083	1.3	2,034	3.2
North Central total:	87,243	0.6	59,885	0.7	50,215	0.8	9,670	1.7
North total:	172,039	0.4	128,060	0.5	94,041	0.6	34,019	1.1
South:								
Southeast:								
Florida	16,147	2.1	11,427	2.4	4,900	3.7	6,527	3.3
Georgia	24,784	1.1	22,440	1.1	14,338	1.3	8,102	2.0
North Carolina	18,447	1.7	15,497	1.9	11,194	2.1	4,303	4.0
South Carolina	12,746	1.8	11,189	1.8	7,320	2.1	3,869	3.5
Virginia	15,766	1.1	13,000	1.2	9,992	1.3	3,008	2.9
Southeast total:	87,889	0.7	73,553	0.7	47,744	0.8	25,809	1.4
South Central:								
Alabama	22,693	1.1	21,264	1.1	14,792	1.3	6,471	2.4
Arkansas	18,830	1.3	15,156	1.4	9,390	1.8	5,767	2.4
Kentucky	11,970	1.5	10,647	1.6	9,103	1.7	1,543	4.8
Louisiana	14,222	1.7	12,512	1.8	5,815	2.5	6,697	2.5
Mississippi	19,622	1.3	17,320	1.3	12,146	1.4	5,174	2.8
Oklahoma	7,665	5.5	7,000	6.0	5,716	7.1	1,283	8.2
Tennessee	14,460	1.5	12,310	1.6	9,975	1.7	2,335	4.2
Texas	17,273	1.2	16,204	1.2	10,841	1.1	5,363	2.7
South Central total:	126,756	0.6	112,412	0.6	77,779	0.8	34,633	1.1
South total:	214,644	0.4	185,965	0.5	125,522	0.6	60,443	0.9

Table B. (continued)

Region, subregion, and state	Public							
	Total		Federal		State		Local	
	Acres	SE [a]	Acres	SE [a]	Acres	SE [a]	Acres	SE [a]
	Thousands	Percent	Thousands	Percent	Thousands	Percent	Thousands	Percent
North:								
Northeast:								
Connecticut	411	14.7	-	-	257	18.5	154	24.3
Delaware	32	40.5	-	-	32	40.5	-	-
Maine	1,098	6.3	164	16.8	776	7.5	158	16.3
Maryland	609	8.7	72	26.5	424	10.3	113	20.6
Massachusetts	992	9.5	106	30.3	603	12.0	283	18.2
New Hampshire	1,204	7.3	773	8.9	265	16.3	166	20.7
New Jersey	810	7.6	106	21.5	531	9.2	173	16.7
New York	4,231	3.8	142	22.8	3,630	4.0	459	12.6
Pennsylvania	4,839	2.8	603	8.4	3,812	3.1	424	10.1
Rhode Island	53	26.7	-	-	42	31.8	10	56.0
Vermont	754	7.8	369	10.9	313	12.2	72	26.2
West Virginia	1,589	5.0	1,233	5.6	278	12.4	77	23.5
Northeast total:	16,621	1.8	3,568	3.7	10,964	2.1	2,088	5.5
North Central:								
Illinois	795	7.9	368	11.1	204	16.0	223	15.6
Indiana	767	7.8	403	10.6	334	11.9	31	40.2
Iowa	327	13.0	104	22.9	163	18.4	60	30.3
Michigan	7,427	1.6	2,958	2.5	4,118	2.1	351	8.1
Minnesota	9,277	1.5	2,789	2.7	4,400	2.1	2,089	3.2
Missouri	2,686	3.7	1,838	4.4	784	7.1	63	25.9
Ohio	921	8.1	276	14.5	423	11.8	222	16.8
Wisconsin	5,157	1.9	1,576	3.5	1,075	4.4	2,506	2.7
North Central total:	27,357	0.9	10,312	1.6	11,501	1.4	5,545	2.1
North total:	43,978	0.9	13,880	1.5	22,465	1.3	7,633	2.1
South:								
Southeast:								
Florida	4,720	4.1	2,068	6.0	2,221	6.0	431	14.3
Georgia	2,343	3.9	1,758	4.4	356	10.2	230	12.7
North Carolina	2,950	4.8	2,090	5.6	601	10.9	258	16.7
South Carolina	1,557	5.6	1,071	6.8	325	12.6	160	17.7
Virginia	2,766	3.0	2,250	3.2	302	9.5	213	11.4
Southeast total:	14,336	2.0	9,237	2.3	3,806	4.2	1,293	6.9
South Central:								
Alabama	1,429	5.4	986	6.5	330	11.4	113	19.6
Arkansas	3,674	3.2	3,155	3.3	446	10.2	71	25.3
Kentucky	1,324	5.3	1,059	5.9	212	13.9	53	28.4
Louisiana	1,709	5.3	975	6.8	538	9.8	197	16.1
Mississippi	2,303	4.2	1,834	4.6	236	13.3	233	13.6
Oklahoma	665	11.6	499	13.4	139	25.8	27	59.0
Tennessee	2,171	4.3	1,473	5.2	599	8.5	99	21.3
Texas	1,069	5.6	905	6.2	109	16.1	54	21.9
South Central total:	14,344	1.7	10,886	1.9	2,611	4.3	847	7.4
South total:	28,679	1.3	20,124	1.5	6,417	3.0	2,139	5.1

Region, subregion, and state	All ownerships		Private					
			Total		Family		Other Private	
	Acres	SE [a]	Acres	SE [a]	Acres	SE [a]	Acres	SE [a]
	Thousands	Percent	Thousands	Percent	Thousands	Percent	Thousands	Percent
Rocky Mountain:								
Great Plains:								
Kansas	2,106	5.0	1,994	5.1	1,906	5.2	88	25.2
Nebraska	1,245	6.8	1,092	7.2	1,054	7.4	38	39.3
North Dakota	724	9.0	510	10.7	424	11.7	86	26.1
South Dakota	1,682	5.9	492	10.9	352	12.9	140	20.5
Great Plains total:	5,757	3.1	4,088	3.7	3,736	3.8	352	12.8
Intermountain:								
Arizona	18,671	2.2	7,381	3.5	1,371	8.4	6,010	3.9
Colorado	22,612	2.1	5,360	5.0	4,193	5.6	1,168	10.9
Idaho	21,430	3.1	2,553	10.2	1,186	15.0	1,367	14.0
Montana	25,014	2.6	7,026	5.1	3,628	7.1	3,398	7.4
Nevada	11,089	4.7	212	36.8	93	55.7	120	49.1
New Mexico	16,682	1.9	6,331	3.1	6,331	3.1	-	-
Utah	17,962	2.0	3,013	5.5	1,941	6.8	1,071	9.2
Wyoming	11,445	2.1	1,942	5.4	1,655	5.8	287	14.3
Intermountain total:	144,905	0.9	33,819	1.9	20,399	2.4	13,420	3.2
Rocky Mountain total:	150,661	0.9	37,906	1.8	24,135	2.1	13,772	3.1
Pacific Coast:								
Alaska:								
Alaska	126,869	1.2	35,875	2.5	4,056	7.3	31,818	2.7
Alaska total:	126,869	1.2	35,875	2.5	4,056	7.3	31,818	2.7
Pacific Northwest:								
Oregon	30,169	1.5	11,059	2.6	4,257	4.2	6,802	3.3
Washington	22,279	1.9	9,806	3.0	2,717	5.6	7,088	3.6
Pacific Northwest total:	52,449	1.2	20,864	2.0	6,974	3.4	13,890	2.4
Pacific Southwest:								
California	32,817	1.4	13,202	2.4	7,897	3.1	5,305	3.8
Hawaii	1,748	9.0	1,155	10.9	1,031	11.5	124	35.5
Pacific Southwest total:	34,565	1.4	14,357	2.4	8,928	3.0	5,429	3.8
Pacific Coast total:	213,883	0.8	71,097	1.5	19,960	2.3	51,137	1.8
United States total:	751,228	0.3	423,029	0.4	263,658	0.4	159,371	0.6

Region, subregion, and state	Public							
	Total		Federal		State		Local	
	Acres	SE [a]	Acres	SE [a]	Acres	SE [a]	Acres	SE [a]
	Thousands	Percent	Thousands	Percent	Thousands	Percent	Thousands	Percent
Rocky Mountain:								
Great Plains:								
Kansas	112	22.3	73	27.6	20	53.5	19	53.9
Nebraska	153	19.6	81	26.8	52	33.4	19	55.3
North Dakota	214	16.5	157	19.3	46	35.5	11	72.5
South Dakota	1,190	7.0	1,138	7.1	52	33.6	-	-
Great Plains total:	1,669	5.9	1,449	6.3	170	16.5	49	34.1
Intermountain:								
Arizona	11,291	2.6	9,658	3.0	1,609	7.7	24	63.7
Colorado	17,252	2.3	16,590	2.3	603	15.2	58	50.0
Idaho	18,877	3.2	17,342	3.3	1,535	13.1	-	-
Montana	17,987	2.9	17,175	3.0	799	15.3	13	120.0
Nevada	10,876	4.7	10,824	4.8	52	74.2	-	-
New Mexico	10,351	2.4	9,522	2.5	825	9.1	3	152.3
Utah	14,950	2.2	13,425	2.3	1,514	7.7	11	90.8
Wyoming	9,503	2.3	9,084	2.3	419	11.8	-	-
Intermountain total:	111,086	1.1	103,620	1.1	7,357	4.4	109	34.8
Rocky Mountain total:	112,755	1.0	105,070	1.1	7,527	4.3	159	26.2
Pacific Coast:								
Alaska:								
Alaska	90,994	1.4	63,423	1.7	27,469	2.7	101	46.1
Alaska total:	90,994	1.4	63,423	1.7	27,469	2.7	101	46.1
Pacific Northwest:								
Oregon	19,111	1.8	17,960	1.8	969	8.7	181	20.6
Washington	12,474	2.5	9,536	2.8	2,580	5.9	358	16.1
Pacific Northwest total:	31,584	1.5	27,496	1.5	3,549	4.9	539	12.7
Pacific Southwest:								
California	19,614	1.8	18,409	1.8	831	10.1	375	15.3
Hawaii	593	15.7	12	114.3	573	16.0	8	141.2
Pacific Southwest total:	20,208	1.8	18,421	1.8	1,404	8.8	383	15.3
Pacific Coast total:	142,786	1.0	109,340	1.1	32,422	2.4	1,023	9.9
United States total:	328,199	0.6	248,413	0.7	68,831	1.3	10,955	2.1

[a] SE = sampling error

Note: Data may not add to totals due to rounding

Table C.--Area and number of private forests in the United States by region, subregion, and state, 2006

Region, subregion, and state	Area		Owners	
	Acres	SE [a]	Number	SE [a]
	Thousands	Percent	Thousands	Percent
North:				
Northeast:				
Connecticut	1,383	7.4	108	21.7
Delaware	351	11.6	55	57.1
Maine	16,575	1.3	252	13.1
Maryland	1,957	4.8	157	24.5
Massachusetts	2,179	5.8	293	18.8
New Hampshire	3,646	3.8	128	23.8
New Jersey	1,322	5.7	122	28.1
New York	14,438	1.9	667	12.9
Pennsylvania	11,738	1.7	497	6.8
Rhode Island	303	10.8	38	29.8
Vermont	3,864	2.7	88	19.2
West Virginia	10,418	1.6	251	22.4
Northeast total:	68,175	0.7	2,677	5.5
North Central:				
Illinois	3,730	3.6	184	13.3
Indiana	3,888	3.2	225	10.8
Iowa	2,552	4.5	150	17.6
Michigan	12,117	1.2	498	9.1
Minnesota	7,114	1.8	202	8.5
Missouri	12,393	1.6	359	7.2
Ohio	6,973	2.6	345	10.0
Wisconsin	11,117	1.2	362	6.8
North Central total:	59,885	0.7	2,325	3.5
North total:	128,060	0.5	5,002	3.4
South:				
Southeast:				
Florida	11,427	2.4	509	22.6
Georgia	22,440	1.1	524	10.9
North Carolina	15,497	1.9	525	12.1
South Carolina	11,189	1.8	301	13.9
Virginia	13,000	1.2	410	13.3
Southeast total:	73,553	0.7	2,269	7.0
South Central:				
Alabama	21,264	1.1	412	11.5
Arkansas	15,156	1.4	346	22.7
Kentucky	10,647	1.6	473	14.5
Louisiana	12,512	1.8	131	17.9
Mississippi	17,320	1.3	370	48.6
Oklahoma	7,000	2.8	71	13.9
Tennessee	12,310	1.6	534	11.6
Texas	16,204	1.2	354	12.0
South Central total:	112,412	0.6	2,690	9.8
South total:	185,965	0.4	4,960	5.4

Table C. (continued)

Region, subregion, and state	Area		Owners	
	Acres	SE [a]	Number	SE [a]
	Thousands	*Percent*	*Thousands*	*Percent*
Rocky Mountain:				
Great Plains:				
Kansas	1,994	5.1	103	18.9
Nebraska	1,092	7.2	57	33.1
North Dakota	510	10.7	24	48.6
South Dakota	492	10.9	12	37.4
Great Plains total:	4,088	3.7	196	15.2
Intermountain:				
Arizona	7,361	3.5	45	40.5
Colorado	5,360	5.0	186	39.1
Idaho	2,553	10.2	34	54.6
Montana	7,026	5.1	40	22.9
Nevada	212	36.8	15	64.1
New Mexico	6,331	3.1	81	81.7
Utah	3,013	5.5	66	59.5
Wyoming	1,942	5.4	24	47.5
Intermountain total:	33,819	1.8	491	22.5
Rocky Mountain total:	37,906	1.7	687	16.7
Pacific Coast:				
Alaska:				
Alaska	35,875	2.5	82	89.3
Alaska total:	35,875	2.5	82	89.3
Pacific Northwest:				
Oregon	11,059	2.6	149	16.8
Washington	9,806	3.0	215	18.9
Pacific Northwest total:	20,864	2.0	364	13.1
Pacific Southwest:				
California	13,202	2.4	202	19.1
Hawaii	1,155	0.2	25	53.5
Pacific Southwest total:	14,357	2.2	227	18.0
Pacific Coast total:	71,097	1.5	673	14.3
United States total:	423,029	0.4	11,322	3.1

[a] SE = sampling error

Note: Data may not add to totals due to rounding

Table D.--Area and number of nonindustrial private forests in the United States by region, subregion, and state, 2006

Region, subregion, and state	Area		Owners	
	Acres	SE [a]	Number	SE [a]
	Thousands	Percent	Thousands	Percent
North:				
Northeast:				
Connecticut	1,383	7.4	106	21.7
Delaware	325	12.0	55	57.1
Maine	12,082	1.5	252	13.1
Maryland	1,669	4.9	157	24.5
Massachusetts	2,179	5.8	293	18.8
New Hampshire	3,451	3.8	128	23.8
New Jersey	1,322	5.7	122	28.1
New York	13,710	1.9	686	12.9
Pennsylvania	11,505	1.7	497	6.8
Rhode Island	303	10.8	38	29.8
Vermont	3,612	2.8	68	19.2
West Virginia	10,418	1.6	251	22.4
Northeast total:	62,158	0.8	2,677	5.5
North Central:				
Illinois	3,725	3.6	184	13.3
Indiana	3,870	3.2	225	10.8
Iowa	2,552	4.5	150	17.6
Michigan	10,986	1.3	498	9.1
Minnesota	6,467	1.9	202	8.5
Missouri	12,234	1.6	359	7.2
Ohio	6,780	2.6	345	10.0
Wisconsin	10,438	1.3	362	6.8
North Central total:	57,055	0.7	2,324	3.5
North total:	119,213	0.5	5,001	3.4
South:				
Southeast:				
Florida	9,652	2.7	509	22.6
Georgia	18,172	1.2	524	10.9
North Carolina	13,969	1.9	525	12.1
South Carolina	9,712	1.9	301	13.9
Virginia	12,256	1.2	410	13.3
Southeast total:	63,762	0.8	2,269	7.0
South Central:				
Alabama	17,765	1.2	412	11.5
Arkansas	10,983	1.7	345	22.7
Kentucky	10,398	1.6	473	14.5
Louisiana	8,250	2.2	131	17.9
Mississippi	15,340	1.4	370	48.6
Oklahoma	5,952	2.9	71	43.1
Tennessee	11,206	1.6	534	11.6
Texas	12,996	1.4	354	41.2
South Central total:	92,891	0.6	2,690	10.9
South total:	156,652	0.5	4,945	6.1

Table D. (continued)

Region, subregion, and state	Area		Owners	
	Acres	SE [a]	Number	SE [a]
	Thousands	Percent	Thousands	Percent
Rocky Mountain:				
Great Plains:				
Kansas	1,994	5.1	103	18.9
Nebraska	1,092	7.2	57	33.1
North Dakota	510	10.7	24	48.6
South Dakota	492	10.9	12	37.4
Great Plains total:	4,088	3.7	196	15.2
Intermountain:				
Arizona	7,381	3.5	45	40.5
Colorado	5,360	5.0	186	39.1
Idaho	1,427	13.7	34	54.6
Montana	5,430	5.6	40	22.9
Nevada	212	36.8	15	64.1
New Mexico	6,331	3.1	81	61.7
Utah	3,013	5.5	66	59.5
Wyoming	1,942	5.4	24	47.5
Intermountain total:	31,097	1.9	491	22.5
Rocky Mountain total:	35,184	1.6	687	16.7
Pacific Coast:				
Alaska:				
Alaska	35,875	2.5	82	89.3
Alaska total:	35,875	2.5	82	89.3
Pacific Northwest:				
Oregon	6,970	3.3	149	16.9
Washington	6,510	3.6	215	18.9
Pacific Northwest total:	13,480	2.5	364	13.1
Pacific Southwest:				
California	10,101	2.7	202	19.1
Hawaii	1,155	15.0	25	53.5
Pacific Southwest total:	11,256	2.9	227	18.0
Pacific Coast total:	60,612	1.7	673	14.3
United States total:	371,661	0.4	11,307	3.3

[a] SE = sampling error

Note: Data may not add to totals due to rounding

Table E.--Area and number of family forests in the United States by region, subregion, and state, 2006

Region, subregion, and state	Area		Owners	
	Acres	SE [a]	Number	SE [a]
	Thousands	Percent	Thousands	Percent
North:				
Northeast:				
Connecticut	898	8.7	101	22.8
Delaware	244	13.7	28	54.3
Maine	5,727	2.2	233	13.8
Maryland	1,462	5.4	156	24.7
Massachusetts	1,686	6.2	290	19.0
New Hampshire	2,358	4.3	124	24.6
New Jersey	805	7.3	120	28.5
New York	11,252	2.0	614	10.8
Pennsylvania	8,906	1.8	469	6.9
Rhode Island	204	12.5	37	30.9
Vermont	3,109	2.8	87	19.3
West Virginia	7,174	1.8	243	23.1
Northeast total:	43,825	0.9	2,502	5.3
North Central:				
Illinois	3,465	3.7	177	13.6
Indiana	3,471	3.4	218	11.1
Iowa	2,449	4.5	147	17.9
Michigan	8,956	1.4	436	4.9
Minnesota	5,390	2.0	194	8.6
Missouri	11,605	1.6	339	7.3
Ohio	5,796	2.7	336	10.2
Wisconsin	9,083	1.3	352	6.9
North Central total:	50,215	0.8	2,201	3.2
North total:	94,041	0.6	4,703	3.2
South:				
Southeast:				
Florida	4,900	3.7	404	20.9
Georgia	14,338	1.3	504	11.1
North Carolina	11,194	2.1	469	11.8
South Carolina	7,320	2.1	262	12.6
Virginia	9,992	1.3	402	13.6
Southeast total:	47,744	0.8	2,042	6.5
South Central:				
Alabama	14,792	1.3	399	11.8
Arkansas	9,390	1.8	343	22.9
Kentucky	9,103	1.7	467	14.7
Louisiana	5,815	2.5	105	17.0
Mississippi	12,146	1.4	163	14.0
Oklahoma	5,716	2.7	52	13.5
Tennessee	9,975	1.7	531	11.7
Texas	10,841	1.2	344	11.9
South Central total:	77,779	0.7	2,403	6.2
South total:	125,522	0.5	4,445	4.2

Table E. (continued)

Region, subregion, and state	Area		Owners	
	Acres	SE [a]	Number	SE [a]
	Thousands	*Percent*	*Thousands*	*Percent*
Rocky Mountain:				
Great Plains:				
Kansas	1,906	5.2	101	19.2
Nebraska	1,054	7.4	54	34.2
North Dakota	424	11.7	24	48.7
South Dakota	352	12.9	12	39.0
Great Plains total:	3,736	3.8	191	15.5
Intermountain:				
Arizona	1,371	8.4	44	41.3
Colorado	4,193	5.6	182	39.8
Idaho	1,186	15.0	34	55.2
Montana	3,628	7.1	38	23.8
Nevada	93	55.6	11	64.1
New Mexico	6,331	3.1	81	81.7
Utah	1,941	6.8	64	62.1
Wyoming	1,655	5.8	24	47.9
Intermountain total:	20,399	2.4	478	23.1
Rocky Mountain total:	24,135	2.1	669	17.1
Pacific Coast:				
Alaska:				
Alaska	4,058	7.3	16	119.3
Alaska total:	4,058	7.3	16	119.3
Pacific Northwest:				
Oregon	4,257	4.2	141	17.4
Washington	2,717	5.8	213	19.2
Pacific Northwest total:	6,974	3.4	354	13.5
Pacific Southwest:				
California	7,897	3.1	197	19.6
Hawaii	1,031	11.5	14	53.5
Pacific Southwest total:	8,928	3.0	210	18.7
Pacific Coast total:	19,960	2.3	581	11.1
United States total:	263,658	0.4	10,398	2.6

[a] SE = sampling error

Family Forest Owners of the United States*, 2006

As with all estimates derived from surveys, sampling errors should be considered when interpreting the results. Estimates with sampling errors of 25 percent or more should be used cautiously. Estimates with sampling errors of 50 percent or more should be used very cautiously.

Citation: Butler, B.J. 2008. Family forest owners of the United States, 2006. Gen. Tech. Rep. NRS-27. Newtown Square, PA: U.S. Department of Agriculture, Forest Service, Northern Research Station.

* Excluding interior Alaska, Hawaii, Nevada, western Oklahoma, and western Texas.

Table US-1.--Number of responses and cooperation rate for family forest owners who participated in the U.S. Forest Services' National Woodland Owner Survey between 2002 and 2006 in the United States*

Surveys sent	Number of undeliverables	Number of responses	Cooperation rate
			Percent
35,121	5,029	15,440	51.3

* Excluding interior Alaska, Hawaii, Nevada, western Oklahoma, and western Texas.

Table US-2.--Area of forest land in the United States* by ownership category, 2006

Ownership category	Area	
	Acres	SE *
	Thousands	Percent
Private		
Family	251,974	0.4
Other private	127,943	0.8
Total private	379,917	1.1
Public		
Federal	185,977	0.8
State	41,964	1.7
Local	10,850	2.0
Total public	238,791	0.7
Total	618,708	0.4

* Excluding interior Alaska, Hawaii, Nevada, western Oklahoma, and western Texas.
* SE = sampling error

Table US-3.—Area and number of private forests in the United States* by size of forest landholdings, 2006

Size of forest landholdings	Area		Owners	
	Acres	SE [a]	Number	SE [a]
Acres	Thousands	Percent	Thousands	Percent
1-9	20,561	7.2	6,821	5.2
10-19	16,475	6.3	1,496	3.7
20-49	42,591	3.4	1,465	2.5
50-99	44,020	3.2	683	2.4
100-199	43,770	3.5	372	4.8
200-499	47,300	3.6	185	3.8
500-999	25,578	5.9	45	5.4
1,000-4,999	42,229	5.0	28	6.3
5,000-9,999	12,677	15.2	2	13.6
10,000+	82,617	2.6	9	47.9
Total	379,917	0.4	11,108	3.2

* Excluding interior Alaska, Hawaii, Nevada, western Oklahoma, and western Texas.

[a] SE = sampling error

Table US-4.—Area and number of nonindustrial private forests in the United States* by size of forest landholdings, 2006

Size of forest landholdings	Area		Owners	
	Acres	SE [a]	Number	SE [a]
Acres	Thousands	Percent	Thousands	Percent
1-9	20,561	7.2	6,821	5.2
10-19	16,475	6.3	1,496	3.7
20-49	42,591	3.4	1,465	2.5
50-99	44,020	3.2	683	2.4
100-199	43,770	3.5	372	4.8
200-499	47,300	3.6	185	3.8
500-999	25,578	5.9	45	5.4
1,000-4,999	42,229	5.0	28	6.3
5,000-9,999	12,677	15.2	2	13.6
10,000+	31,249	6.6	8	54.9
Total	326,549	0.4	11,107	3.2

* Excluding interior Alaska, Hawaii, Nevada, western Oklahoma, and western Texas.

[a] SE = sampling error

Table US-5.--Area and number of family forests in the United States* by size of forest landholdings, 2006

Size of forest landholdings	Area		Owners	
	Acres	SE [a]	Number	SE [a]
Acres	Thousands	Percent	Thousands	Percent
1-9	19,158	6.4	6,221	4.4
10-19	17,691	6.5	1,430	3.7
20-49	40,894	3.4	1,402	2.5
50-99	41,562	3.2	644	2.3
100-199	38,946	3.5	318	2.6
200-499	39,926	3.7	158	4.2
500-999	16,795	7.0	32	5.3
1,000-4,999	25,127	5.8	18	8.8
5,000-9,999	4,217	19.8	1	11.6
10,000+	5,659	18.3	<1	21.0
Total	251,974	0.4	10,223	2.7

* Excluding interior Alaska, Hawaii, Nevada, western Oklahoma, and western Texas.

[a] SE = sampling error

Table US-6.--Area and number of family forests in the United States* by percent of owner's land that is forested, 2006

Percent forested	Area		Owners	
	Acres	SE [a]	Number	SE [a]
	Thousands	Percent	Thousands	Percent
<25	30,435	4.7	2,557	7.2
25-49	39,291	4.1	1,392	7.2
50-74	51,909	3.3	2,402	7.4
75-99	74,217	2.5	1,536	4.7
100	46,154	3.8	1,889	8.0
No answer	9,968	11.0	348	15.8

* Excluding interior Alaska, Hawaii, Nevada, western Oklahoma, and western Texas.

[a] SE = sampling error

Table US-7.--Area and number of family forests in the United States* by number of forested parcels, 2006

Forested parcels	Area		Owners	
	Acres	SE [a]	Number	SE [a]
	Thousands	Percent	Thousands	Percent
1	77,319	2.1	4,159	4.2
2-9	92,429	1.9	2,088	5.4
10-99	13,605	9.0	89	12.2
100+	1,701	30.4	4	22.0
No answer	66,721	2.5	3,882	4.7

* Excluding interior Alaska, Hawaii, Nevada, western Oklahoma, and western Texas.

[a] SE = sampling error

Table US-8.—Area and number of family forests in the United States[*] by type and source of forest land acquisition, 2006

Acquisition	Area		Owners	
	Acres	SE [a]	Number	SE [a]
	Thousands	Percent	Thousands	Percent
Type [a]				
Purchase	191,380	1.0	6,259	3.2
Inheritance	66,616	2.2	1,994	6.1
Other	14,723	6.9	511	15.1
No answer	5,400	19.5	183	17.2
Source [b]				
Family	123,005	1.6	3,333	4.9
Individual	141,961	1.4	5,594	3.8
Other	25,589	5.8	1,411	10.7
No answer	7,577	14.6	371	14.8

[*] Excluding Interior Alaska, Hawaii, Nevada, western Oklahoma, and western Texas.

[a] SE = sampling error

[b] Categories are not exclusive.

Table US-9.—Area and number of family forests in the United States[*] by ownership tenure, 2006

Land tenure (years)	Area		Owners	
	Acres	SE [a]	Number	SE [a]
	Thousands	Percent	Thousands	Percent
<10	30,567	4.4	1,891	6.9
10-24	67,704	2.5	3,330	5.2
25-49	87,157	2.2	2,998	5.9
50+	21,832	6.4	480	11.9
No answer	44,714	3.9	1,524	7.5

[*] Excluding Interior Alaska, Hawaii, Nevada, western Oklahoma, and western Texas.

[a] SE = sampling error

Table US-10.--Area and number of family forests in the United States* by frequency and recipient of forest land transfers, 2006

Land transfer	Area		Owners	
	Acres	SE [a]	Number	SE [a]
	Thousands	Percent	Thousands	Percent
Frequency				
0 (never)	163,757	1.2	7,525	3.3
1	38,914	4.0	1,683	8.6
2-5	28,806	5.0	572	10.3
6+	11,259	11.5	79	30.1
No answer	9,237	14.0	364	13.9
Recipient [b]				
Family	23,466	4.9	620	12.6
Individual	45,890	2.8	1,302	8.5
Other	21,623	4.9	540	18.6
No answer	7,066	11.9	239	16.7
Transferred in last 5 years				
Yes	39,921	3.1	1,079	9.8
No	203,214	0.7	8,821	3.1
No answer	8,840	8.3	323	13.4

* Excluding interior Alaska, Hawaii, Nevada, western Oklahoma, and western Texas.

[a] SE = sampling error

[b] Categories are not exclusive.

Table US-11.--Area and number of family forests in the United States* by form of ownership, 2006

Form of ownership [a]	Area		Owners	
	Acres	SE [b]	Number	SE [b]
	Thousands	Percent	Thousands	Percent
Individual or joint	207,400	0.9	9,286	3.3
Family partnership	40,506	4.2	631	12.9
Trust	22,974	6.6	367	11.3
Other	7,354	13.8	167	33.0
No answer	3,945	23.8	232	28.3

* Excluding interior Alaska, Hawaii, Nevada, western Oklahoma, and western Texas.

[a] Categories are not exclusive.

[b] SE = sampling error

Table US-12.--Area and number of family forests in the United States* that are associated with owners' farms, primary homes, and vacation homes, 2006

Associated with *	Area		Owners	
	Acres	SE [b]	Number	SE [b]
	Thousands	Percent	Thousands	Percent
Owner's farm				
Yes	100,030	1.7	2,389	5.3
No	143,767	1.2	7,521	3.3
No answer	8,177	12.7	313	14.4
Owner's home (primary residence)				
Yes	139,160	1.3	7,054	3.4
No	95,379	1.8	2,598	5.5
No answer	17,435	7.5	572	10.2
Owner's vacation home or cabin				
Yes	48,766	3.2	1,078	7.5
No	176,246	1.0	8,145	3.1
No answer	26,961	5.3	1,000	8.1

* Excluding interior Alaska, Hawaii, Nevada, western Oklahoma, and western Texas.

* Categories are not exclusive.

[b] SE = sampling error

Table US-13.--Area and number of family forests in the United States* by reason for owning forest land, 2006. Numbers include landowners who ranked each objective as very important (1) or important (2) on a seven-point Likert scale.

Reason *	Area		Owners	
	Acres	SE [b]	Number	SE [b]
	Thousands	Percent	Thousands	Percent
To enjoy beauty or scenery	160,601	1.1	7,159	3.4
To protect nature and biologic diversity	130,403	1.4	5,489	3.7
For land investment	117,868	1.5	3,852	5.0
	128,868	1.6	6,649	4.0
Part of home or vacation home				
Part of farm or ranch	102,265	1.9	2,865	6.0
Privacy	135,474	1.3	6,362	3.4
To pass land on to children or other heirs	150,918	1.2	4,960	3.8
To cultivate/collect nontimber forest products	25,212	5.2	753	8.4
For production of firewood or biofuel	37,667	3.8	1,274	6.6
For production of sawlogs, pulp-wood or other timber products	78,634	2.0	1,023	5.7
Hunting or fishing	109,928	1.6	2,682	4.9
For recreation other than hunting or fishing	84,963	2.0	2,899	5.2
No answer	2,967	26.7	127	22.2

* Excluding interior Alaska, Hawaii, Nevada, western Oklahoma, and western Texas.

* Categories are not exclusive.

[b] SE = sampling error

Table US-14.--Area and number of family forests in the United States* by lease status, 2006

Leased	Area		Owners	
	Acres	SE [a]	Number	SE [a]
	Thousands	Percent	Thousands	Percent
Yes	55,429	3.0	515	8.3
No	165,359	0.9	9,229	2.9
No answer	11,166	10.6	479	13.6
Use [b]				
Hunting	17,344	7.7	60	11.4
Recreation (other than hunting)	7,822	14.6	46	16.3
Graze/pasture livestock	17,349	7.8	184	16.7
Timber production	7,570	14.7	56	17.7
Cultivate/collect nontimber forest products	4,607	19.5	33	16.1
Other	1,017	53.4	5	27.5
No answer	24,586	5.2	221	12.3
Leased within past 5 years				
Yes	41,039	3.8	278	10.9
No	194,046	0.9	9,392	2.9
Uncertain	597	78.4	6	46.4
No answer	16,290	8.0	546	12.1

* Excluding interior Alaska, Hawaii, Nevada, western Oklahoma, and western Texas.

[a] SE = sampling error

[b] Categories are not exclusive.

Table US-15.--Area and number of family forests in the United States* by status of easements that restrict land use conversions**, 2006

Easement	Area		Owners	
	Acres	SE [a]	Number	SE [a]
	Thousands	Percent	Thousands	Percent
Yes	8,629	11.6	171	14.1
No	227,609	0.6	9,389	2.9
No answer	15,536	8.0	663	10.1
Future easement [b]				
Yes	3,079	25.8	65	26.9
No	108,450	1.6	5,147	4.1
Maybe	36,383	3.9	1,146	7.0
Uncertain	30,276	4.4	1,144	7.1
No answer	49,621	3.3	1,887	7.1

* Excluding interior Alaska, Hawaii, Nevada, western Oklahoma, and western Texas.

** Despite our intention of quantifying conservation easements, many respondents included rights-of-way and other easements and their answers should be interpreted accordingly.

[a] SE = sampling error

[b] Includes only owners who currently do not have an easement.

Table US-16.--Area and number of family forests in the United States* by knowledge of and participation in sustainable forest certification programs, 2006

Green certification	Area		Owners	
	Acres	SE [a]	Number	SE [a]
	Thousands	Percent	Thousands	Percent
Has heard of				
Yes	56,909	2.7	1,206	7.5
No	182,657	0.9	8,497	3.0
No answer	12,408	9.5	519	11.2
Land currently enrolled [b]				
Yes	10,490	9.6	82	12.8
No	43,169	3.4	991	6.9
No answer	3,250	26.7	136	43.2
Enroll land in future [c]				
Yes	1,209	48.5	14	30.9
No	17,524	6.8	573	10.4
Maybe	12,402	8.2	196	13.7
Uncertain	4,351	22.2	92	19.9
No answer	7,682	13.4	116	10.7

* Excluding interior Alaska, Hawaii, Nevada, western Oklahoma, and western Texas.

[a] SE = sampling error

[b] Includes only owners who have heard of green certification.

[c] Includes only owners who have heard of green certification and who currently do not have land green certified.

Table US-17.--Area and number of family forests in the United States* by participation in cost-share programs, 2006

Cost-share program	Area		Owners	
	Acres	SE [a]	Number	SE [a]
	Thousands	Percent	Thousands	Percent
Yes	48,909	3.2	526	8.7
No	188,631	0.9	9,043	2.9
No answer	14,434	8.4	652	11.3
Participated in past 5 years				
Yes	24,839	5.5	218	14.0
No	210,390	0.7	9,347	2.8
Uncertain	1,282	49.3	28	55.6
No answer	15,453	8.2	631	11.4

* Excluding interior Alaska, Hawaii, Nevada, western Oklahoma, and western Texas.

[a] SE = sampling error

Table US-18.--Area and number of family forests in the United States* by primary forest management decisionmaker, 2006

Primary decisionmaker [a]	Area		Owners	
	Acres	SE [b]	Number	SE [b]
	Thousands	Percent	Thousands	Percent
Owner	214,897	0.7	9,236	2.9
Family member	27,426	5.3	614	13.6
Forester	26,600	4.6	192	9.0
Other	14,994	7.9	185	10.4
No answer	5,519	18.7	209	20.7

* Excluding interior Alaska, Hawaii, Nevada, western Oklahoma, and western Texas.

[a] Categories are not exclusive.

[b] SE = sampling error

Table US-19.--Area and number of family forests in the United States* by timber harvesting activities and reasons, 2006

	Area		Owners	
	Acres	SE [a]	Number	SE [a]
	Thousands	Percent	Thousands	Percent
Trees harvested or removed				
Yes	170,717	1.0	4,543	3.3
No	76,687	2.2	5,414	4.3
No answer	4,570	17.9	266	20.3
Products harvested [b]				
Sawlogs	118,744	1.5	1,891	3.9
Veneer logs	40,778	3.5	515	5.9
Pulpwood	74,407	2.0	1,048	6.8
Firewood	67,374	2.4	1,951	4.7
Posts or poles	29,091	5.4	335	8.8
Other	4,034	21.9	158	20.6
No answer	17,044	7.4	1,059	8.9
Received professional consultation [c]				
Yes	75,538	2.2	1,118	5.8
No	85,347	2.0	3,075	4.3
Uncertain	3,010	27.7	88	23.9
No answer	6,822	13.9	262	14.8
Recent harvest/removal (within 5 years)				
Yes	94,271	1.9	2,043	5.0
No	145,407	1.2	7,665	3.4
Uncertain	2,203	32.5	90	25.5
No answer	10,093	10.6	425	12.2
Commercial harvest [d]				
Yes	135,801	1.3	2,454	4.0
No	99,129	1.7	6,710	3.7
No answer	17,044	7.4	1,059	8.9
Reason for harvest [c]				
Part of management plan	61,341	2.8	685	7.4
Trees were mature	95,225	2.0	1,571	4.5
Clear land	19,187	7.7	733	10.1
Needed money	40,774	3.9	741	7.5
Wood for personal use	41,163	4.0	1,294	5.7
Price was right	32,816	4.5	439	9.7
Improve hunting	18,317	7.4	188	9.7
Improve recreation	11,137	10.8	308	11.6
Remove trees damaged by natural catastrophes	64,020	2.9	1,745	6.3
Improve quality of remaining trees	83,122	2.2	1,708	5.8
Other	7,875	16.1	313	15.7
No answer	10,782	9.8	569	11.3

* Excluding interior Alaska, Hawaii, Nevada, western Oklahoma, and western Texas.

[a] SE = sampling error

[b] Categories are not exclusive.

[c] Includes only owners who have harvested.

[d] A commercial harvest is defined as the harvesting of sawlogs, veneer logs, or pulpwood.

Table US-20.—Area and number of family forests in the United States* by activities related to nontimber forest products (NTFPs), 2006

	Area		Owners	
	Acres	SE [a]	Number	SE [a]
	Thousands	Percent	Thousands	Percent
NTFPs collected or harvested				
Yes	54,989	3.2	1,701	6.1
No	180,572	1.0	7,856	3.4
No answer	16,413	7.8	667	14.9
Type of NTFPs collected/harvested [b,c]				
Edibles	30,522	4.9	1,005	6.8
Medicinals	6,865	15.3	215	20.1
Decoratives	21,254	6.8	728	10.3
Cultural	2,044	41.6	27	24.4
Other	644	66.6	34	44.2
No answer	12,329	7.6	285	15.3
Use [b,c]				
For sale	10,273	12.4	163	20.5
For personal use	36,259	4.3	1,319	6.9
No answer	12,919	7.5	297	14.9
Recent (within past 5 years)				
Yes	37,457	4.3	1,239	7.3
No	186,532	1.0	8,041	3.3
Uncertain	747	64.3	18	28.1
No answer	27,237	4.8	925	11.7

* Excluding interior Alaska, Hawaii, Nevada, western Oklahoma, and western Texas.

[a] SE = sampling error

[b] Categories are not exclusive.

[c] Includes only owners who have collected nontimber forest products.

Table US-21.--Area and number of family forests in the United States* by management plan status, 2006

Management plan	Area		Owners	
	Acres	SE [a]	Number	SE [a]
	Thousands	Percent	Thousands	Percent
Yes	42,367	3.5	364	7.2
No	197,059	0.8	9,393	2.9
Do not remember	4,561	19.5	131	18.2
No answer	7,986	13.1	336	17.4

* Excluding Interior Alaska, Hawaii, Nevada, western Oklahoma, and western Texas.

[a] SE = sampling error

[b] Categories are not exclusive.

Table US-22.--Area and number of family forests in the United States* by recent (past 5 years) forestry activity, 2006

Activity [a]	Area		Owners	
	Acres	SE [b]	Number	SE [b]
	Thousands	Percent	Thousands	Percent
Timber harvest	61,610	2.2	1,125	5.0
Collection of NTFPs [c]	37,457	4.3	1,239	7.3
Site preparation	40,677	3.5	822	9.1
Tree planting	65,701	2.3	1,920	5.5
Fire hazard reduction	50,936	3.1	1,294	8.1
Application of chemicals	38,917	3.6	928	9.1
Road/trail maintenance	90,056	1.9	1,685	6.5
Wildlife habitat improvement	51,518	3.0	857	7.7
Posting land	107,169	1.9	2,366	5.7
Private recreation	135,309	1.5	3,329	4.3
Public recreation	36,855	4.4	711	12.6
None of the above	41,343	3.5	3,181	5.6

* Excluding Interior Alaska, Hawaii, Nevada, western Oklahoma, and western Texas.

[a] Categories are not exclusive.

[b] SE = sampling error

[c] NTFPs = nontimber forest products

Table US-23.—Area and number of family forests in the United States* by advice received and advice source, 2006

	Area		Owners	
	Acres	SE [a]	Number	SE [a]
	Thousands	Percent	Thousands	Percent
Advice received				
Yes	91,468	1.9	1,436	5.7
No	153,493	1.1	8,504	3.1
No answer	7,013	14.8	284	18.5
Advice source [b]				
State forestry agency	45,308	3.4	548	7.0
Extension	16,687	7.5	238	15.4
Other state agency	4,267	21.7	53	16.8
Federal agency	22,982	6.1	263	11.3
Private consultant	42,300	3.4	354	8.0
Forest industry	13,060	8.0	75	9.4
Logger	17,667	6.8	220	12.9
Another landowner	16,987	6.8	269	14.1
Other	2,763	28.7	114	29.7
No answer	9,381	11.7	351	16.0

* Excluding interior Alaska, Hawaii, Nevada, western Oklahoma, and western Texas.

[a] SE = sampling error

[b] Categories are not exclusive.

Table US-24.—Area and number of family forests in the United States* by preferred methods to receive forest management information, 2006. Numbers include landowners who ranked each method as very useful (1) or useful (2) on a seven-point Likert scale.

Method [a]	Area		Owners	
	Acres	SE [b]	Number	SE [b]
	Thousands	*Percent*	*Thousands*	*Percent*
Publications, books, or pamphlets	107,594	1.8	3,822	4.5
Newsletters, magazines, or newspapers	91,275	2.1	3,210	5.2
Internet/web	50,146	3.4	2,402	6.4
Conferences, workshops, or video conferences	39,102	4.3	975	10.1
Video tapes for home viewing	55,621	3.1	2,207	6.5
Television or radio programs	43,339	3.7	1,848	7.1
Visiting other woodlands or field trips	50,236	3.2	1,372	7.4
Talking with a forester or other natural resource professional	116,243	1.7	3,246	5.0
Talking with other woodland owners	66,698	2.6	1,633	6.5
Talking with a logging contractor	35,169	4.6	813	10.1
Membership in a land owner organization	33,812	4.8	739	8.8
No answer	13,489	8.7	713	11.0

* Excluding interior Alaska, Hawaii, Nevada, western Oklahoma, and western Texas.

[a] Categories are not exclusive.

[b] SE = sampling error

Table US-25.—Area and number of family forests in the United States* by landowners' sociopolitical concerns, 2006. Numbers include landowners who ranked each issue as a very important (1) or important (2) concern on a seven-point Likert scale.

Concern [a]	Area		Owners	
	Acres	SE [b]	Number	SE [b]
	Thousands	Percent	Thousands	Percent
Dealing with an endangered species	66,269	2.8	2,307	6.8
High property taxes	128,970	1.5	4,978	4.2
Keeping land intact for heirs	140,890	1.4	4,622	4.1
Lawsuits	73,169	2.6	2,286	6.1
Regulations that restrict harvesting	75,693	2.5	2,237	7.6
Development of nearby lands	82,092	2.3	3,785	4.8
Damage or noise from motorized vehicles	65,686	2.8	3,112	5.3
Trespassing or poaching	130,388	1.5	4,560	4.2
Timber theft	66,876	2.6	2,512	6.0
Misuse of forest land, such as vandalism or dumping	116,651	1.7	4,608	4.3
No anwer	9,043	11.4	521	15.5

* Excluding interior Alaska, Hawaii, Nevada, western Oklahoma, and western Texas.

[a] Categories are not exclusive.

[b] SE = sampling error

Table US-26.—Area and number of family forests in the United States* by landowners' forest health concerns, 2006. Numbers include landowners who ranked each issue as a very important (1) or important (2) concern on a seven-point Likert scale.

Concern [a]	Area		Owners	
	Acres	SE [b]	Number	SE [b]
	Thousands	Percent	Thousands	Percent
Air or water pollution	86,191	2.0	4,349	4.7
Undesirable plants	84,141	2.2	3,243	5.0
Domestic animals	22,529	6.2	1,026	10.7
Wild animals	37,491	4.0	1,614	6.4
Fire	132,164	1.5	4,916	4.5
Insects or plant diseases	140,848	1.4	4,945	4.1
Lack of new trees	46,274	3.5	2,373	6.6
Wind or ice storms	89,918	2.0	3,740	5.3
No answer	10,187	10.4	526	12.2

* Excluding interior Alaska, Hawaii, Nevada, western Oklahoma, and western Texas.

[a] Categories are not exclusive.

[b] SE = sampling error

Table US-27.--Area and number of family forests in the United States* by landowners' future (next 5 years) plans for their forest land, 2006

Future plans [a]	Area		Owners	
	Acres	SE [b]	Number	SE [b]
	Thousands	Percent	Thousands	Percent
Leave it as is - no activity	73,167	2.3	4,303	4.4
Minimal activity to maintain forest land	97,169	2.0	3,352	4.6
Harvest firewood	66,358	2.4	1,978	4.3
Harvest sawlogs or pulpwood	63,034	2.5	716	6.7
Collect nontimber forest products	19,465	6.8	569	9.5
Sell some or all of their forest land	18,420	6.9	550	14.4
Give some or all of their forest land to heirs	41,588	3.8	903	6.4
Subdivide some or all of their forest land and sell subdivisions	5,775	17.3	118	21.4
Buy more forest land	31,859	4.4	699	10.1
Convert some or all of their forest land to another use	8,914	12.0	253	15.7
Convert another land use to forest land	7,492	12.8	157	17.7
No current plans	37,781	4.3	1,949	8.0
Unknown	13,574	9.1	651	14.1
Other	10,002	11.8	289	14.6
No answer	6,196	14.3	276	16.2

* Excluding interior Alaska, Hawaii, Nevada, western Oklahoma, and western Texas.

[a] Categories are not exclusive.

[b] SE = sampling error

Table US-28.--Area and number of family forests in the United States* by primary occupation of the primary decisionmaker, 2006

Occupation	Area		Owners	
	Acres	SE [a]	Number	SE [a]
	Thousands	Percent	Thousands	Percent
Farmer	21,965	7.3	445	23.2
Official or manager	23,314	6.5	906	15.6
Professional	25,875	6.1	1,079	11.0
Technician	841	49.9	92	43.7
Sales worker	7,203	13.5	299	18.0
Administrative support	3,515	21.5	243	23.8
Craft worker	10,662	9.9	716	13.5
Operative	7,544	12.6	443	13.8
Laborer or helper	3,388	23.7	101	22.8
Service worker	3,176	22.1	277	22.6
Homemaker	2,809	25.4	124	28.1
Other [b]	646	56.1	47	39.5
Retiree	120,002	1.9	4,672	5.4
No answer	21,035	7.3	778	12.0

* Excluding interior Alaska, Hawaii, Nevada, western Oklahoma, and western Texas.

[a] SE = sampling error

[b] Includes students, disabled, and unemployed individuals.

Table US-29.--Area and number of family forests in the United States* by age of the primary decisionmaker, 2006

Age (years)	Area		Owners	
	Acres	SE [a]	Number	SE [a]
	Thousands	Percent	Thousands	Percent
<35	2,774	25.7	229	29.3
35-44	15,035	7.5	894	9.0
45-54	46,503	3.2	2,179	5.7
55-64	68,065	2.7	3,169	6.5
65-74	56,792	3.2	1,867	6.4
75+	46,866	3.8	1,487	6.8
No answer	15,939	8.4	396	12.1

* Excluding interior Alaska, Hawaii, Nevada, western Oklahoma, and western Texas.

[a] SE = sampling error

Table US-30.--Area and number of family forests in the United States* by highest level of formal education of the primary decisionmaker, 2006

Highest level of education	Area		Owners	
	Acres	SE [a]	Number	SE [a]
	Thousands	Percent	Thousands	Percent
12th grade or lower	18,871	6.7	1,046	9.3
High school or equivalent	55,902	2.6	2,624	5.5
Some college	43,183	3.5	1,882	6.1
Associate's degree	20,888	6.5	1,156	9.9
Bachelor's degree	53,437	3.0	1,550	7.1
Graduate degree	43,165	3.6	1,438	7.1
No answer	16,528	7.5	525	12.3

* Excluding interior Alaska, Hawaii, Nevada, western Oklahoma, and western Texas.

[a] SE = sampling error

Table US-31.--Area and number of family forests in the United States* by primary decisionmaker's annual household income, 2006

Income	Area		Owners	
	Acres	SE [a]	Number	SE [a]
	Thousands	Percent	Thousands	Percent
Less than $25,000	26,017	5.6	1,474	7.8
$25,000 - $49,999	54,847	3.1	2,573	6.3
$50,000 - $99,999	69,883	2.6	3,134	5.0
$100,000 - $199,000	34,460	4.6	1,278	10.3
$200,000 or more	21,183	6.0	301	13.8
No answer	45,565	3.8	1,464	7.8

* Excluding interior Alaska, Hawaii, Nevada, western Oklahoma, and western Texas.

[a] SE = sampling error

Table US-32.--Area and number of family forests in the United States* by gender of the primary decisionmaker, 2006

Gender	Area		Owners	
	Acres	SE [a]	Number	SE [a]
	Thousands	Percent	Thousands	Percent
Male	183,503	0.9	7,013	3.3
Female	33,757	4.3	1,640	6.2
Both [b]	19,352	6.6	1,072	9.6
No answer	15,262	8.2	498	13.1

* Excluding interior Alaska, Hawaii, Nevada, western Oklahoma, and western Texas.

[a] SE = sampling error

[b] Respondent indicated joint decisionmakers, at least one male and one female.

Table US-33.–Area and number of family forests in the United States* by ethnicity and race of the primary decisionmaker, 2006

Ethnicity and race	Area		Owners	
	Acres	SE [a]	Number	SE [a]
	Thousands	Percent	Thousands	Percent
Ethnicity				
Hispanic or Latino	3,333	32.2	110	33.6
Non-Hispanic/Latino	220,343	0.8	9,116	3.1
No answer	28,298	5.5	998	9.2
Race				
People reporting a single race				
American Indian or Alaska Native	1,203	48.3	56	42.3
Asian	429	78.7	17	46.6
Black or African American	1,731	29.9	163	22.9
Native Hawaiian or other Pacific Islander	209	102.2	32	60.0
White	224,885	0.7	9,116	3.1
Two or more races	4,494	19.8	217	17.6
No answer	19,024	7.6	623	12.6

* Excluding interior Alaska, Hawaii, Nevada, western Oklahoma, and western Texas.

[a] SE = sampling error

Table US-34.–Area and number of family forests in the United States* by disability of the primary decisionmaker, 2006

Disability	Area		Owners	
	Acres	SE [a]	Number	SE [a]
	Thousands	Percent	Thousands	Percent
Vision or hearing				
Yes	19,536	6.4	712	9.5
No	212,366	0.7	8,945	3.2
No answer	20,072	6.9	566	10.7
Physical (e.g., mobility)				
Yes	40,340	4.0	1,584	7.2
No	191,444	0.9	8,074	3.3
No answer	20,190	6.9	566	10.3

* Excluding interior Alaska, Hawaii, Nevada, western Oklahoma, and western Texas.

[a] SE = sampling error